# HEALING *Where You* HURT

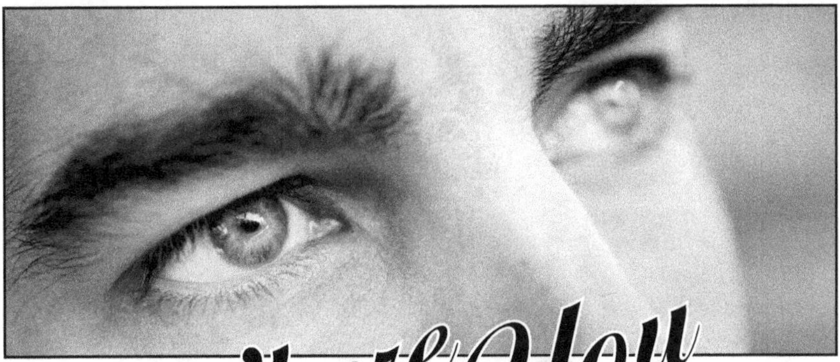

## ... ON THE INSIDE

**Jon Eargle**

**Healing Where You Hurt ... On the Inside**
by Jon Eargle

Copyright © 2019 JON EARGLE MINISTRIES, INC. Eighth Printing, 2019

All rights reserved. No portion of this book may be used in any form without the written permission of the author with the exception of brief excerpts in magazine articles, reviews, etc. For permission to use any larger portion of this book and related teaching, please contact permissions editor at joneargleministries.org.

ISBN 978-0-9790251-5-0

Printed in the United States

Scriptures marked KJV are taken from the KING JAMES VERSION (KJV): KING JAMES VERSION, public domain.

Scriptures marked NIV are taken from the NEW INTERNATIONAL VERSION (NIV): Scripture taken from THE HOLY BIBLE, NEW INTERNATIONAL VERSION ®. Copyright© 1973, 1978, 1984, 2011 by Biblica, Inc.™. Used by permission of Zondervan

Scripture quotations taken from the New American Standard Bible® (NASB), Copyright © 1960, 1962, 1963, 1968, 1971, 1972, 1973, 1975, 1977, 1995 by The Lockman Foundation. Used by permission. www.Lockman.org

Published by VisionRun.com

# TABLE OF CONTENTS

| | Page |
|---|---|
| Foreword | 5 |
| Preface  Healing: Our Heritage in Christ | 7 |
| Ch. 1  Healing on the Inside | 11 |
| Ch. 2  Responding, Rather Than Reacting | 25 |
| Ch. 3  Overcoming Anger, Resentment, and Bitterness | 45 |
| Ch. 4  How to Conquer Your Fears | 57 |
| Ch. 5  How to Forgive and Then Forget | 77 |
| Ch. 6  The Rage of Self-Pity | 87 |
| Ch. 7  Defeating Depression | 105 |
| Ch. 8  How to Do Inner Healing with Yourself | 121 |
| Inner Healing Glossary | 131 |
| Appendix A  Victory in Your Thought Life | 133 |
| Appendix B  How to be Born Again—Spiritually | 135 |
| Appendix C  For Additional Resources | 139 |
| End Notes | 140 |

*This book is lovingly dedicated to*

MY WIFE, CATHIE, and CHILDREN, TODD and LISA
*who have endured me in all my ups and downs,
reaffirming me in my pilgrimage of self-discovery.*

# FOREWORD

*We still remember the day vividly. We had spent several hours with Jon, talking, sharing and praying with him about inner healing. Then, as he was getting ready to leave, the Lord gave a prophecy saying that He was calling this Baptist preacher into the healing ministry and would anoint him and use him in a glorious way.*

*Praise the Lord, the prophecy was, indeed, from the Lord. Jon has been used greatly and through this book is bringing more insight to the inner healing ministry.*

*God wants all His children to be WHOLE: spirit, soul, and body. This book will help in the search for wholeness. It will enlighten, inform, and inspire!*

*— Ed & Betty Tapscott*

# FOREWORD

"Prayer visioning" is a term I had never heard before. I was well acquainted with the process whereby prayer counselors prayed with other people through the hurts of early life. This is commonly called "inner healing." I had practiced it in my own ministry with good results but prayer visioning, as Jon expressed it, was something new; it had become a startlingly effective way of God's letting people see or experience what Jesus was doing to complete the healing of emotional wounding. In prayer the Holy Spirit allows one to see or sense what Jesus is doing to heal even the most desperate problems — rape — incest - parental abuse and homosexuality.

Jon has clearly shown that hurts and rejection can go back to the fetal period. His own childhood was so physically bruising that it is something of a marvel he has been able to survive emotionally at all. For six months he lived on the savage edge of suicide — praying daily for God to allow him to die. Then God spoke to him and promised him that over a period of time he would experience his healing. God miraculously healed him and launched him into a nation-wide ministry that has helped people from almost every state.

This book chronicles some dramatic stories of God's gracious healing power — the man who had molested all four of his daughters and has remained healed — the rape cases healed in one session — the many people afflicted with depression who have been set free. It will set your heart a'singing to know God still heals the emotionally ill.

But that is not the main purpose of the book. It is a how-to book, Jon's consuming desire is to help you receive your own inner healing — for we all need to be healed. This book is unique in that it can help you, step by step, to understand why you feel the way you do — and how to apply the three-fold principles of confession, forgiveness, and prayer visioning, to your own life situation. No one will read this book without gaining more self-understanding more insight into God's ways of healing, and without meeting himself on page after page.

— Dr. Charles Farah, Professor of Theology Oral Roberts University

# PREFACE

She lay limp and unmoving — like a rag doll. It had happened so many times before. She had cried out, but no one had come, and they wouldn't now. It continued from the time she was six years old until she was twelve, and pregnant. Her daddy would come home drunk and angry and she was always the victim — the only one he would rape. The seventh child in a poor, minority family, she had never been wanted, not during the pregnancy, her birth, nor a single day since.

When it first began, she would cry out for her mommy, or one of her older brothers and sisters, but no one came. They could not, would not hear — they were too afraid. Twelve and pregnant, the neighbors became alarmed and notified the police. The father was arrested, convicted and sentenced to thirty years in prison, but still she was not wanted. Her family now blamed her for causing daddy to be taken away. They wanted nothing more to do with her, after all, she was the cause of all their problems.

She was made a ward of the court, passed among several foster homes and under psychological care for three years, but with little real improvement. At times she would awaken screaming in the night — the nightmare of daddy had returned. She would lie there crying, whimpering, lonely and afraid (thank God for some foster parents by now who cared and tried to reach out in love!).

I remember the first time they brought her to me. They were in a van and it was 11:30 p.m. when I began to pray for a pretty little fifteen year old girl, huddled in her foster mother's arms sobbing and whimpering, remembering — trying to forget. I know how to pray, and pray with authority, but after thirty minutes I remember feeling that I had been able to accomplish so very little in comparison to the need. There were severe, traumatic memories that must be healed if she were ever to be set free to live anything like a normal life, but praise God that He can heal those hurting memories and He is doing so with her.

Healing is part of our heritage as Christians. Jesus' entire ministry revolved around healing of one kind or another. His biblical names included Counselor, Redeemer, and Great Physician.

*Healing Where You Hurt*

The Bible is replete with references concerning healing. The heart of God throbs with His desire to heal our hurts and meet our needs. "I pray that in all respects you may prosper and be in good health, just as your soul prospers," III John 2 (NASB). "Heal me, O Lord, and I will be healed," Jeremiah 17:14 (NASB). "I will restore you to health and I will heal you of your wounds, declares the Lord," Jeremiah 30:17 (NASB). "Surely He hath borne our griefs and carried our sorrow," Isaiah 53:4 (KJV). "By His stripes ye are healed," Isaiah 53:5. "For I know the plans I have for you, declares the Lord, plans for welfare and not calamity to give you a future and a hope," Jeremiah 29:11 (NASB). He promises healing in Exodus 15:26, I Peter 2:24, Proverbs 3:5-9, Proverbs 4:20, 22.

The welfare which God promises in Jeremiah refers to all three areas of man's being. The Bible teaches us that man is a trinity. He is spirit, soul and body (1 Thess. 5:23). Jesus' death on the cross has already provided healing in each of these three basic areas (1 Peter 2:24). Not one area or the other, but in each!

## HEALING FOR OUR SPIRIT

Healing for our spirit is what we receive in the new birth experience. It is the beginning of salvation in the total sense, but traditionally we have referred to it as healing of the spirit or soul. The church has usually used these two terms as synonymous. I believe they are not. While "spirit" and "soul" are many times used interchangeably, the term "soul" basically refers to the area of the mind and emotions. In conversion it is the spirit which is recreated. (II Cor. 5:17) I believe that "soul winning" as it has been used traditionally is not a biblical term because it does not refer to the initial experience of conversion, but rather to the ongoing renewal of the mind or soul area.

## HEALING FOR OUR BODY

There is no way to understand the ministry of Jesus apart from the concept of healing for the whole person: spirit, soul and body. What a loss when the church began to limit its ministry to only the area of "spiritual things" as if God is concerned only for some vague ethereal something that will be with Him in heaven.

God cares about people. Jesus ministered to people. He touched people. He wept over people. He died for people! How tragic when His church becomes preoccupied with either philosophical proofs (or concerns) or religious statistics. To the degree that a local church is really the Church, it will be oriented to meeting the needs of people in the name and power of Jesus, just as He was!

All my prayers for healing used to be qualified with the pious phrase "thy will be done". This seemed to me to be the epitome of spiritual submission. Then a simple analogy changed my entire healing theology. When I would go to a doctor, I always assumed that he wanted me well and would do everything possible to make it so (no matter what kind of man he was, or whether he cared about me personally or not). But I approached my loving, caring heavenly Father with doubt and unbelief. I wasn't sure whether He wanted me well or not. "Maybe He wants me to stay sick — for punishment or to teach me something."

Then it dawned upon me. If a man who might not even know me, or care about me, and who might not even be a believer, wanted me well, how much more did my loving Father? This is the meaning and message of Matthew 7:7-11. "How much more shall your Father who is in heaven give what is good to those who ask Him!" (NASB) Even the psalmist of centuries ago affirmed "No good thing does He withhold from those who walk uprightly".

Try to remove physical healing from the ministry of Jesus as it is related in the New Testament, and you will have to tear out most of the pages of the gospels. Take the Gospel of Mark, for example. Over and over and over again you find phrases like "and He healed many. . .," "Be made whole ..." and "Take up your bed and walk ..."

It was a primary means for Him to show His love and to cause people to believe. Is it any less so now? Does He love us any less? God forbid! (And it was not simply a sign for unbelievers as some would teach today.) Repeatedly I see how easy it is to reach one for Christ when one ministers to his needs as when he helps him where he hurts.

The book of Acts shows us that the early Christians had the same ministry. After all, isn't this the way Jesus said it would be in John 14:12? Nowhere do I read that He has revoked either His commission (Mark 16:17-18) or His promise. As the scripture says, He is "the same yesterday, today and forever," Hebrews 13:8.

## **HEALING FOR OUR SOUL**

While conversion of the spirit is instantaneous (initiating us into salvation), the "saving of the soul" is a process. The Old Testament terminology is "restoring the soul" (Psalms 23:3), while the New Testament speaks of "renewing the mind" (Romans 12:2). They both refer to a remodeling process. The soul or mind of the believer has to be renovated. God has to cleanse us of the world's philosophies and renew our minds with His perspective. This comes basically through the Word of God — the Bible. We must live in it until it lives in us.

It is my personal belief that there are five basic areas of the mind in regard to its healing. There are the thought processes, the emotions, the imagination, memories and the will. In many ways this is a more critical area of healing than the body. Satan's attacks on the Christian almost always seem to be initiated in this area. (The real battle is for men's minds.) He comes against us in our thought processes and then his attack spreads to our emotions, flashes a picture on the screen of our imagination and begins to replay tapes from our memories of similar past experiences. Before we realize it, the initial temptation to think wrongly (detrimentally and in a self-defeating way) has grown from a molehill into the proverbial mountain. It can ravage us like a prairie fire.

No wonder we need inner healing! We must learn to "take every thought captive in obedience to Christ" (II Corinthians 10:5). The screen of our imagination must have a new set of photographs and with our memories old things must pass away so that all can become new. Through Christ we must come into controlling us, and our will must be released from its bondage to the things of the world so that we can have will power.

Without, healing in this area we can never really conform to the image of Christ (Romans 8:29). Most of our physical problems grow out of our mental and emotional hurts and hang-ups (and we all have them — it is just a matter of degree). How will we ever get the things of God deep into our inner man (our spirit) if our mind is continually congested with the opposite viewpoint? It must be cleansed and healed for us to ever be made whole.

Healing on the inside is imperative to the victorious Christian life. It is essential to getting off the emotional roller coaster. It is what will allow us to be "more than conquerors," or overcomers. And this is the area in which every believer must be an overcomer.

Thus, the remainder of this book will basically deal with this one subject of healing on the inside — inner healing through the healing of memories. For that is where we all have hurts that hinder our experiencing the abundant life and that short-circuit God's plan for our lives.

*Chapter 1*

# HEALING ON THE INSIDE

Is anyone 98.6° emotionally? No. Everyone hurts some on the inside. The difference is only a matter of degree, and God knows this so much better than we do. There is no need that we have with which God is not concerned, and no hurt which we have experienced that He does not desire to heal. There is no area of our lives that He does not want to touch and make whole.

## *Pain Does Not Hurt*

God wants to heal us where we hurt — on the inside. He is not content merely to minister to our symptoms. He does not want simply to remove our pain. In a very real sense pain does not hurt. It only lets us know that we are hurting. Pain is like a smoke alarm. It alerts us to the fact that our "house" is on fire somewhere. Pain informs us that there is a short-circuit in our system — physically or emotionally. It is not meant to be a negative, but a positive.

We make a basic mistake when we simply pray for God to take away the pain. That's like shutting off the smoke alarm and going back to bed while the house continues to burn. We must learn to discern, treat and pray for the root cause of the problem. The pain is designed to help point us in the right direction. It is a warning signal to let us know there is a problem — to cause us to slow down, to correct habits and to deal with problems rather than running from them.

## *Treating Symptoms, Not Root Causes*

Too many times both medicine and counseling tend merely to treat symptoms without ever dealing with the root cause. "Have a headache? Take two aspirin and lie down for twenty minutes." Sure it tends to help temporarily, but nothing has been done about what caused the headache. Thus, the same problem will simply reoccur again and again. It is time for us to get tough about pain. We need to understand its role in God's plan for us and begin to listen to what it is saying. Indeed, to begin to realize that our pain is frequently a gift from God. A loving gift to capture our attention so that we will not have to continue hurting, but can begin to wait before Him and to understand what our bodies and emotions are trying to say. Then, when we hear, we can reach out and receive healing.

Through the process of inner healing, God can show us the memories which are at the root of our hurts and begin to heal us once and for all. Time is no barrier to the Lord, so He can even heal us retroactively. Hebrews 13:8 (NIV) says, "Jesus Christ the same yesterday, today and forever." No matter where the root, He can ferret it out and remove it. He can take us through time today into our yesterdays and heal hurts just as in His resurrection appearance to the apostles when he passed through the wall without ever opening the door. Time is not a dimension in the spiritual life.

## *An Example of Root Healing*

A session with a woman comes to mind. Her heart was bursting. She had so many hurts, they just poured out. In silent prayer I said, "Lord, do what only you can do. Stop the flow of emotion now that only makes her hurt all over again and bring to the surface the memories which you want to heal."

As God's peace began to come in and she became quiet, I told her we were ready to ask God to begin to heal her. We had prayer together, and immediately He brought to her mind a key experience that happened when she was a small child. Her daddy had come into the room. He looked at her mother and said, "I want a divorce. I don't love you any more." Since that moment she had felt rejected by her father. She loved him very much. He was dead now but still the rejection was there, and it has been transferred to her husband. God healed the little girl inside of her that day. He told her that her father had not rejected her, but only her mother. Then Jesus just held her and loved her and allowed His healing to soak in more deeply. She left so differently than she had arrived. God's healing touch is beautiful to behold.

## *Recognize the Need*

For God to be able to do this kind of healing there must be a deep sense of our need for it. He can't heal us until there is. We must believe that we need to be healed, as a non-Christian must know that he needs to be saved. Psalm 142:7 reads, "Bring my soul out of prison so that I may give thanks to thee." Remember that the "soul" is basically the mind area and consists of five aspects: thought, will, emotions, memories, and imagination. If our thoughts and emotions are unhealed, it's like being in prison, and that prison is always with us, no matter where we go. We could take the greatest vacation in the world, go to Hawaii and stay in the finest hotel, eat the best food and buy everything our hearts desired. We could do anything, go any place on those islands that we wanted to go, but the hurts down inside could still make us miserable. It happens all the time. We are prisoners of ourselves.

## Our Main Enemy

We really only have two enemies. One is our adversary, the devil. The other is our own selves. Those are the only enemies we have — and the devil is limited in what he can do to us. So we really have one primary foe — ourselves. As Pogo once said, "We has met de enemy, and he is us!" If we can realize the problem is within ourselves and that God knows it and wants to heal and correct it, then we can be set free. Psalm 119:175 (KJV) says, "Let my soul live that it may praise thee". Let my soul come alive! Let me have that abundant life that God intended for me, so that I may praise Him! You can really be released to praise Him when you know you've been healed and forgiven.

Another important insight is found in III John 2. The New American Standard reads, "Beloved, I pray that in all respects you may prosper and be in good health, just as your soul prospers". It is saying that when your soul is not healthy, it affects your prosperity, and the health of every other area in life. Much physical illness is due to the need for healing in the emotional and mental areas. All doctors acknowledge this. It' been estimated that anywhere from 60-90% of all physical ailments are a result of the need for emotional healing. God is saying to us, "I want you to prosper and be in good health but I want you to know that it is directly related to the prosperity of your soul." The starting point of all healing is really with our spirit, but this is a word to believers whose spirits have already been reborn.

## Healing the Little Child

Jesus taught that to enter the Kingdom of God, one must become as a little child. This is the only way to enter into God's family. Thus, if the Kingdom of God is to come into us, we must become as a little child, but for the Kingdom to come OUT of us (be manifested through our lives), the little child in us must be healed. Otherwise we will remain childish adults, whether Christians or not. Unhealed childhood hurts cause us to behave childishly in that area of our lives as adults. This is why there are more childish Christians that there are child-like ones.

The real turning point in my life began in April, 1978. I attended a Healing Ministries Workshop here in Tulsa. During that time I began to become very aware of my need for emotional healing. As the conference progressed my subconscious emotions were stirred up more and more. I hurt and ached almost as if I had the flu. I cried readily. By mid-week I knew I must speak to someone to obtain help in understanding what was happening inside of me. I decided to try to speak to Tommy Tyson, a conference leader who had spoken most on this thing called inner healing. It was crushing to find that he had left the day before to return to his home. My emotional turmoil continued to worsen. On that final day I wrestled with speaking to Francis MacNutt, the workshop director, but didn't. My tears flowed like a river through the final session on Friday night and I did not know why. All I knew was that I was in deep emotional turmoil. Complete exhaustion set in. On Saturday I awakened to a phone call and then went back to sit on the bed. An intense pain began to grow inside my abdomen. It increased until I was doubled over, crying like a baby. The pain was as intense as the pain from a kidney stone, which I had had some years before. I cried out in my agony for God to do something, to tell me what was occurring! Instinctively I knew it was emotion and not physical. Minutes seemed like hours.

## A Vision From God

Suddenly I began to "see" something. I thought it was in my "mind's eye," but have since realized it was in my spirit. Today I would call it a vision, but not then. There was a surgical operation room with a man on the operating table. Two doctors and a team of assistants were in the room. One of the doctors took his scalpel and cut open the man's abdomen. I couldn't see anything bloody or gory, but I knew what was happening. Then the strangest thing occurred. The doctor laid down his scalpel and turned to walk from the room. The second one did the same, and was followed by all the other attendants. The man was lying on the operating table with his stomach cut wide open, and everyone was walking away. He began to scream, "My God, my God, don't do this to me! Come back, don't leave me like this! At least come back and sew me up!"

By this time I was sobbing uncontrollably, and the pain was tremendous. Slowly it began to subside. God said, "Do you understand, my son? You're the one on the operating table. You went to this seminar and the teaching on inner healing opened you up emotionally. The first surgeon was Tommy Tyson. His teaching cut you open, but he seemed to walk away without even sewing you up.* You contemplated on Friday talking to Francis MacNutt, but you never did. Now it's Saturday and the seminar is over, and he has gone home, too. All the other team members have left, also. Everyone is gone and your insides feel like they are falling out!" Then God said, "You can do one of two things. You can push it back down inside and sew yourself back together, so to speak, and most people will never know how you hurt inside because they will never really know you that well, but you'll know. You will know that you could have been healed and whole, but you chose not to be. Or you can let me continue the process of inner healing and set you free. "But, remember," He said, "there is no healing without pain." (Though the pain of inner healing is really as nothing compared to going year after year still hurting.) Then there was nothing. No picture and no sound. Only stark silence, as the abdominal pain subsided. A weird compulsion grew within me. There was an almost overwhelming desire to sit on the floor with my back up against the side of the bed — draw my knees up into my chest, wrap my arms around them, and rock back and forth crying like a baby. It was almost more than I could control, but I knew my wife would be home in a few minutes, and would not be able to handle walking into the room and seeing me that way. So I sat on the side of the bed and did it!

I thought, "My God, that's like some little child!" and He said, "That's right, my son. It is like a little child, because it's not the 42-year-old man that hurts like this. It's the little child in you, and it's the little child that I must heal to set the man free."

## **Healing is a Process**

So I chose to let God heal me and it's been a process. It has been like peeling the layers of an onion. I flew to Houston and had one session with Ed and Betty Tapscott (those dear, anointed saints) and received some healing. The most crucial thing I received was a knowing. I came to know that inner healing was for real and within it lay my liberation. I came back deeply determined to pay whatever the cost required to be set free from the haunting memories of past hurts. I spent two to four hours in the Word of God each morning for nearly three months, searching for answers and prostrating myself before the Lord. He began to reveal and pull down strongholds and to surface significant negative memories for healing. It was a difficult, but glorious time which still continues, for inner healing is a life style.

Psychiatrists and psychologists have said that every experience which we have ever had has molded our personality, causing us to act the way we do. Anything significant that has ever happened to us affects us to some degree. Our subconscious mind has total recall of everything meaningful. The fact that God can bring any of this to the surface is essential to our inner healing, even in the fetal period. Many times in counseling sessions God takes us all the way back to the fetal experience to show us the root of rejection, sometimes into the first few days or months after birth. Almost without exception the root of the problems originated in the pre-school years, or before. What happened then may not actually have been as traumatic as what has happened since, but the little child is basically without emotional defenses or understanding. He has only one way to deal with the feeling of rejection emotionally. He buries it in his subconscious, covers it over, and tries to pretend it didn't happen (this is what we often mean by forgetting). But hurts are meant to be healed, not buried. When they are not, they become infected and will worsen over the years.

It is my conviction that everyone needs inner healing. Everyone has hurts. The difference between us is merely one of degree, and no one is 98.6° emotionally. This includes everybody, no matter how they appear on the surface.

Let me use some descriptive phrases to describe what inner healing is, as I understand it. Inner healing is the healing of broken relationships. It is the changing of bad experiences into good ones, of negative experiences into positive ones. It takes place under the leadership of the Holy Spirit, to be what God created us to be, the real me — the real you. It is the experience of coming to love and accept ourselves as God loves and accepts us, so that we can come to love and accept others the way He does. And, oh, what a difference it makes in the quality of living! It helps make possible the abundant life that Jesus desires for us — that most Christians never really experience to any appreciable degree.

## *God's Love Brings Self-Love*

Until we know how much God loves and accepts us, we can't really love and accept ourselves, and until that takes place, we can't really love and accept others, as God intends. It begins with a new birth because we must be born again. And it continues as we let Him heal us in every area until more and more we become whole as He is whole. In Matthew 5:48 (KJV) Jesus said, "Be ye perfect even as your Father in heaven is perfect". And the word perfect is better translated "to be completely mature". That's what wholeness is, complete maturity. This is His desire for us, too.

How do we obtain such a level of maturity? Many things are involved. Spiritual rebirth is the beginning, but only that. After all, the new birth is simply the beginning of becoming like Jesus, isn't it? It is a birth! It is not an adult experience; it is a child's experience. It is the beginning of spiritual childhood. We make a tragic mistake thinking that if we get someone converted or born again, that's all that is necessary! We think they ought to be fully mature Christians. One of the reasons many think that is because so many doing the teaching are not much more spiritually mature than the ones they are leading to Christ. They only know how to teach on elementary matters, which is insufficient (Hebrews 6:1, 2).

Our spiritual maturity is greatly facilitated by inner healing, which tears down our walls and opens up our understanding. God has many ways of doing this inner healing. Conversion brings healing in both the spirit and soul areas, but it is only the beginning. Confession and forgiveness are vital to any deep inner healing. The filling of the spirit and walking in the spirit continues and extends this inner healing process.

## *Pulling Down Strongholds*

Also, essential to our healing is learning how to pull down strongholds. One of the greatest needs in the church today is to wake up to the fact that we are in spiritual warfare. We are in spiritual warfare. The majority of Christians have no real understanding or conception of what spiritual warfare is, let alone that they are in it all the time. But the Bible is replete with references to it, as in Ephesians 6:12 where Paul says, "we do not wrestle with flesh and blood but we wrestle against principalities and powers, with spiritual forces." And II Corinthians 10:3-5 is a tremendously important passage. It talks about the fact that the warfare we are in is not simply human warfare, and we must not attempt to fight it using only human weapons. That is what we try to do. We must use the "divinely powerful" weapons which God has provided. People are not our primary problem; "principalities and powers" are, and we can't overcome them physically or mentally.

In verse 4, Paul talks about pulling down strongholds. A spiritual stronghold is a strong hold which Satan has in a specific area of one's life spiritually or emotionally. It cannot be broken simply through willpower. It has become a compulsion and it must be cast down by the power of God. A person says, "I can quit drinking any time I want to quit," but he can't because his will cannot be effectively exercised in that area. It is a spiritual stronghold that has to be broken and there are different ways to break it. Inner healing is one of the ways to break it. Inner healing is one of the ways to break a stronghold. Seemingly the only way, many times. Frequently a stronghold can be broken by confession and faith. That's the way God broke seven strongholds in my life in June, 1978, but there were several months of spiritual preparation before I understood how to cooperate with Him in it.

## *Healing Through Prayer Visioning*

For the remainder of this first chapter, I want to concentrate on one basic aspect or method of inner healing which I call Prayer Visioning. It is counseling in a spirit of prayer, in the flow of the Spirit, letting God bring to the surface the key memories that are hurting and binding us, and then allowing us to see or sense in the Spirit what He is doing to heal them. It is similar to what He did through the prophet Elisha with his servant Gehazi in II Kings 6:16-17.

Let me give you an example of the first prayer visioning experience that I consciously had back in April, 1978, prior to my visiting the Tapscotts for inner healing. I was in the recliner in my den telling God how badly I needed to know whether inner healing was valid, or not. I said, "Father, you know the fears I have of going to someone and opening myself up, laying my heart bare, not even knowing what is down inside me. Maybe nothing will come out, or what if they can't really help me and I just hurt that much more? Houston is 500 miles away, and I am so afraid! Please help me. Please heal something in me, and show me that inner healing is for real." Then I heard God say,* "You know your fear, of heights and falling? I'm going to heal it."

I had known it only too well for 25 years. It had emotionally devastated and embarrassed me again and again. The problem had its roots in my last year of high school. We went on our senior trip in May, 1954. Part of the trip was to a state park where there was a bluff several hundred feet high. We had used a back pack trail on the back side to reach the top where you could see for miles. My buddy and I decided it would be "fun" to climb down the face of the cliff though we knew nothing about mountain climbing and had no equipment at all.

I recall that there was about 100 feet of 25-30° incline composed of loose dirt and gravel, and then it was a sheer drop of 500 feet to the boulders and river below. About two-thirds of the way down that 100-foot slope, I lost my footing, fell down and began rolling toward the edge. My hands clung desperately to a patch of grass as my feet dangled towards the abrupt edge overlooking the river some 500 feet below! To say that I was terrified is a great understatement. In the lingo of south Texas, I was "scared spitless!" My mouth was dry as cotton, and I was screaming for help at the top of my voice! Slowly, but surely, the grass was pulling loose from the weight of my body, as my friend sought frantically to get a hand to me and pull me up. From that moment on, I had a fear of falling. For 25 years it haunted me and embarrassed me. All my fighting to overcome it was unsuccessful. It periodically devastated me. My only inroad at all was to learn to fly on an airliner without being wiped out emotionally.

*Chapter 1: Healing on the Inside*

## *A Miraculous Healing*

Then one afternoon in early April, 1978, that changed. In a matter of moments God healed me of that terrible fear, and it has not bothered me since. I was sitting in my recliner in the den, my eyes were closed and God began to give me a vision of what He was doing to heal it. I didn't do anything. I didn't try to see anything, but there I was again hanging on the mountainside. Then another person appeared walking down that steep incline. It was Jesus, and He was walking just like He was on level ground. He walked over to me, reached down and took my hand. He lifted me up and we walked away hand in hand, just like we were walking on level ground. Then it was over. The picture or vision was gone, but there was this beautiful peace inside of me. "Lord, is it really healed after all these years? Just like that?" I hadn't tried to visualize anything. I had never experienced anything like it. I had mixed emotions, and my mind could not comprehend it, but I knew something had happened. God had healed me in a matter of moments and set me free of that terrible, humiliating fear!

Inner healing through the healing of a memory by the use of prayer visioning is a simple, beautiful process in the flow of God's spirit where Jesus brings to the surface of one's conscious mind those areas that hurt and does whatever is necessary to heal them. He does it supernaturally and is always loving and gentle with the person being healed. He knows what we are ready for, and what we can receive as well as exactly what is needed to set us free. There are hundreds of examples that I could give. Let me share only a few.

Sometime ago a woman came for inner healing. She had recently moved to Tulsa, after failing in four marriages. She had two sons and was alienated from both of them. Never had she been able to have a meaningful relationship with a significant male. She talked for some time, pouring her heart out, and then we prayed, asking God to bring to her conscious mind those memories He wanted to heal.

## *A Pretty Pink Dress*

She was a very pleasant woman, of average physical appearance, but felt less attractive than she was. She was a tall, large-boned lady and self-conscious of it. As a child, she never really felt pretty like most girls, because she was bigger and ganglier. More homely, she thought. The first experience that God brought to her mind occurred when she was seven years old. She was walking the two or three miles to school down an old country road, wearing a new pink dress with a pocket in it. (I remember wondering at the time, "What difference does it make whether it has a pocket or not?" but God was soon to show us why.) She felt pretty for one of the few times in her life. The dress was pretty so she felt pretty. It had rained the night before and periodic puddles dotted the road's surface. A car was approaching from the rear and as it reached her its wheel hit a puddle and splashed muddy water all over her pretty pink dress. The memory of it devastated her all over again as she began to sob convulsively. She no longer felt pretty — the mud on her dress made her feel ugly again.

After she regained some composure, we thanked the Lord for bringing it to mind and asked Him to heal it. In prayer we went back to that moment, and I saw someone walking up the road towards her. I said "Do you see someone walking up behind you?" and she said, "Yes". I said, "Can you see who it is?" and she said, "Yes, it's Jesus!" (Now this woman didn't really believe God loved her. She had had so many problems, so much heartache, and heartbreak. She didn't really believe that Jesus loved her, even though she was a Christian. You see, to the degree that we are unhealed inside, to the degree that we have experienced rejection from key people like our parents in our life, to that degree we tend to sense and feel rejection from God. After all, if He really cared, wouldn't He do something to help? We can't really know how much He loves us.) So Jesus came walking towards her and I said to her, "Can you see where He's walking?" She said, "Yes", and I said "Where?" She said "He's walking between me and the mud puddle." (I had been seeing the same thing.) I said, "Do you see the car now?" She said, "Yes, it's coming . . . here it comes." She said, "There, it hit the puddle." She cried out, "Do you know what happened? All the mud went on Jesus, none of it got on me! He took my mud upon Himself."

Again the tears began to flow, but this time they were tears of joy! I could have told her all day long theologically about how Jesus took her sins upon himself, but it would only have been empty words. That day a seven-year-old girl saw Jesus take the mud on Himself, and for the first time in her life, she really knew God loved her. He loved her enough to let her be pretty, and not get the mud on her new pink dress. The two of them hugged and loved each other (that is when a counselor just sits there and doesn't say anything —just praises God!)

Then I saw the most beautiful thing happen. I saw that little girl, who until then, hadn't believed that God really loved her (and didn't really love God, because we can only return God's love; we can't initiate it), reach down into the pocket of her pink dress and take out a handkerchief and begin to wipe the mud off of Jesus! (Then I knew why the pocket was important!) For the first time in her life, she said she felt like she had done something for Him. The simple healing of that deeply hurting memory began to unlock the door to all God's promises for her.

## *Root of Resentment*

A little later God brought back a memory of when she was about two years old. She had a little baby brother, a 15-month-old toddler. She had her little rag dolly in her hand. Her little brother came up and, as a little brother might do at that age, he grabbed at the dolly and accidentally knocked it out of her hand under the dresser. Such a simple little experience it seems on the surface, but again she began to sob convulsively. She was having a terrible trauma, and I knew that what her little brother had done represented a deep hurt inside of her. There had to be much deeper implications. So we prayed and asked God to show us what they were, it became obvious that she hated her brother. She had hated him all his life. Never had she been able to verbalize it because she felt so terrible about it. Do you know why she hated him? This was the story that came out. Her mother nearly died during his birth. They were poor and there were few medical facilities. An infection came in during his birth which left her mommy weak and sick for months. She could not care for this little girl and a single aunt kept her for the next eight or nine months. There was no touch or affection in that relationship. She was literally love-starved. The only companion and security she had during those awful months without her mommy was her little rag doll. It was only a short while after she returned home when this little brother pulled the dolly out of her hand. By this time she had grown to hate her little brother, because in her childish perspective she thought her mother nearly died because of him. It was his fault. And this little girl that needed her mommy so much at that point in her life felt that if it hadn't been for her little brother, she wouldn't have been separated all those months from her mommy.

As this began to unravel, the hatred for men came to the surface. It was obvious why she had never been able to have a successful marriage, why she couldn't even really love her own two sons, yet she had never understood why. So this is what God did. He took us back to her brother's birth. There we were in the room with her brother about to be delivered. Do you know who the doctor was? It was Jesus, the Great Physician. He lovingly and tenderly delivered that little baby brother, but because the Great Physician was there, the infection that came against her mother's body withered and died at the touch of Jesus. So she never became sick. The two problems that had haunted and hurt her all of her life, her mother nearly dying in the childbirth of her brother and the infection that came in and caused the separation from her mother, never occurred. Thus, miraculously, the negative results were removed — in minutes. Don't ask me how that can be healed as if it never happened, but it was. Psychologically it is known that if you can replace a negative experience with a positive one, and if it's done properly, that negative experience will lose its emotional hold on the person. Now that's psychological and it requires time, repetition, and the power of repeated suggestion. What God did took only 3-4 minutes and was done once and for all. God can do in moments what psychology can only do less effectively over an extended period of time. Isn't it wonderful that we don't have to understand it to be able to receive it?

## *Journey into Wholeness*

Man can be used, but only God can give those kind of results. I could share hundreds and hundreds of examples with you of God healing almost every kind of hurt imaginable — rejection, fears, drug addiction, alcoholism, divorce, child abuse, rape and incest. Wholeness is part of our inheritance in Christ. We are heirs of God; we're joint heirs with Jesus. We are heirs of the blessings of Abraham. We have been set free from the curse of the law. There's so much in those three or four biblical statements. Biblically, God wants us to have an abundant life, a rich, full, over-flowing life. Very few people ever have that kind of life. But God wants it for us. We didn't get like we are overnight and our hurts probably won't all be healed overnight. But, when compared to the years it took to build up the hurts, the healing may seem like it happened overnight. Wholeness is a pilgrimage. It's a journey, but I know of nothing more exciting than that journey into wholeness. God wants to heal you where you hurt, and that's on the inside.

Lay the book down, if you will, and let's go to our Father in prayer right now — with all our hurts (Matthew 11:28-30).

## *An Inner Healing Prayer*

Father, you know exactly where everyone who reads this book is emotionally and where they hurt. You know their need and can do for them what no one else can do. Heal them where they hurt, on the inside. Heal those who have experienced rejection even in the fetus because they weren't wanted, and sensed it, those who never heard a daddy's voice exclaim with excitement, "The baby moved, did you see it?", and who never felt a daddy's touch on their mother's stomach to feel that movement, those who never heard the happy expressions of an elated mother and father-to-be who couldn't wait for their child's birth. For each of you who experienced rejection in the womb, in the name of Jesus, I confess that His healing arms of love are reaching out to hold you, and to love you, and to minister to all of your needs.

For each of you who in the trauma of child-birth — the noise, the lights, the sounds — experienced fear which has grown until now your lives have become filled with fear of every kind and description, I confess that Jesus' healing love and strength and presence is driving out that fear and bringing healing release.

To each of you who failed to receive a mother's love in those early months and years, the touch of her body against yours, the feeling of her warmth, love, and affection, for each of you who hungers for that love because you did not have it for any reason, I release Jesus' unconditional love to come in to your inner being, to seep in and saturate your very soul, so that the soaking of that love would heal you and set you free.

For each of you whose daddy was too busy and who did not spend the time with you which you needed, particularly in those formative pre-school years, I ask the healing presence of Jesus to come in and touch and anoint and heal every hurt in this area.

I rebuke the spirits of rejection, fear of rejection, self-rejection and low self-image that have plagued so many of you for so long, and I bind them in the name of Jesus and cast them out. I loose His love in your lives that you might come to see and accept and love yourself as God does. As God's Word declares in John 17:29, the Father loves you as much as He loves His son Jesus and He delights in you.

For every negative experience in your childhood and in those school years of being hurt, embarrassed, rejected, misunderstood, or improperly and falsely accused, in every situation that was mishandled by a teacher (in most instances not intentionally), for every one of those hurts, touch those wounds and heal them.

All of you husbands and wives whose marriages have been a shallow, hollow, empty shell of what God desires for you, I confess His healing love and redemptive power to begin to redeem your relationship and restore it by his resurrection power! I pray that right now with open heart and mind and spirit you will begin to receive your healing. I confess in the name of Jesus that He is healing you and giving you wholeness by the power of Almighty God — beginning this very moment, as you begin to believe and receive.

Thank you Lord. Amen.

*Chapter 2*

# RESPONDING, RATHER THAN REACTING

When pressure builds up inside it must come out somewhere. Many times it expresses its presence by causing us to react, rather than our being able to respond to an irritating situation. As the internal pressure increases we find our emotions controlling us more and more, instead of our controlling them. Most of us are baffled when we find ourselves strongly over-reacting to a situation. Many times we are devastated by the guilt which we feel afterwards. "How could I do that? What made me explode that way? I can't believe I could have said such things!"

## *The Logic of the Emotions*

Outbursts which seem so unexplainable and even out of character have a logical cause. In fact, there is a logical cause and result relationship in every thing we feel and do emotionally. The emotions are not illogical; they simply have a logic of their own. Just as we cannot always understand the logic of the spirit through the logic of the intellect, neither can we properly interpret every action of the emotions through the eyes of the intellect.

The counseling in our ministry center revolves around what I call our Inner Healing Reactions Chart. This chart (which is inserted at the end of this chapter) is a real gift from God. Not in that He dropped it from the sky, but in that He revealed the truths it contains. Over a period of nearly a year God revealed more and more of the logic of the emotions to me.

The chart does not deal with normal emotional responses to a given situation, but rather with abnormal reactions (or over-reactions) where the immediate situation simply triggers a reaction from within our subconscious. Our response, than, is disproportionate to what is happening. There is too much anger, fear, etc. We overreact.

## *Rejection is the Root*

It is my deep conviction that the root of all such reactions is rejection. Continuing experiences of rejection over a period of time will create a sense of rejection in us.

This sense of rejection may develop at any point from the fetus to the recent past, but appears in most instances to be rooted in the pre-school years. When it has taken root, as it continues to grow in its grip on our emotional life, we will begin to develop a fear of rejection. This, then, distorts our perspective, causing us to feel more rejection than we are actually experiencing. So we begin to become more cautious with and suspicious of others, and to create protective emotional walls to insulate ourselves from additional hurt and rejection. This will eventually lead to self-rejection and finally a low self-image.

## *We Bury Our Hurts*

As these emotional processes develop and grow within us, they increase our tendency to try to bury or repress the memory of these hurts and to make ourselves forget them. The solution is not to be found in the treating of the surface symptoms, but in understanding the root cause of our problems and allowing God to do inner healing. This kind of emotional healing invariably requires the healing of memories so that we can be set free again to respond, rather than to react. The chart (with proper explanation and application) is designed to facilitate this greatly. It is a tool for allowing Jesus to show us where the significant hurts are and to aid us in going back into those hurting memories and seeing (or sensing) Jesus healing them through the three-step process we use. It is also designed to show us that our emotions follow a logical progression, and when properly understood, are basically predictable and preventable. They are not a hodge-podge of confusion, but the product of a cause and result relationship which is more intricate than complex.

## *A Reactions Chart*

Let's look at the chart itself now (see pages 42 and 43). The key word in the title is the word "Reactions" because properly understanding the chart depends on your understanding the difference between a reaction and a response. Let me explain what I mean using anger as an example. If a person has a normal response of anger, it means basically two things: our anger is proportionate to the situation and it doesn't last too long. We can deal with it pretty easily, and we don't become more angry than the situation warrants. But when anger is a "reaction," the anger is greater than the situation calls for, and it is increasingly difficult to bring under control. Frequently we just end up pushing it back down inside again. Have you ever had that kind of experience? You find yourself getting much more upset than you should. Sometimes even in the midst of the situation you realize, "Hey, I shouldn't be this upset. It's not that big a deal! Why am I so angry? Why am I so mad?!" The reason is that we are "reacting" rather than "responding."

## *Reactions are Triggered*

Why do we react? Because the situation that occurred has triggered and released anger that was stored inside of us from previous, similar hurting experiences. We appear far more upset than warranted because all this previous upset has been brought into play by our memory bank. Like a row of dominoes the new irritation triggered a chain reaction. We are upset, but not at what has just occurred. Coming to understand the difference between a response and a reaction can make a great deal of difference in the way we are able to handle the situation. When someone is reacting, it means he is that upset, but he is not that upset with us. He is simply that upset inside. When we come to realize this, we don't have to take his reaction so personally, and we can begin to depersonalize and defuse the situation. What usually happens is that we start getting upset because the other person is so upset. We become defensive and react back. We start getting mad because he is so mad at us. What happens then is a reaction to a reaction, which is like two billy goats butting heads. We must learn to break the cycle.

Here's an insight that can help to defuse the situation when someone is reacting to you. If he is more upset than the situation warrants, remind yourself he is reacting, not responding. Then know that when someone reacts, probably 75 to 80% of the anger he is expressing isn't directly related to what you've just done. Maybe 20 to 25% of it relates to you and the situation. It will vary depending on how much anger is coming out, how much is built up in him, and what has happened, but the majority of it will not be directly related to you. Realize that "he's not that mad at me, he's just that mad inside." You don't have to take the explosion personally, because his anger relates more to what is inside of him than what you've just said or done.

## *Trying Too Hard*

The degree of reaction is directly related to the kind and depth of the hurts which we have inside of us. There are only certain things that trigger the reaction. I did not have the kind of relationship with my father which I needed to have. There was a lack of physical and emotional affection. I was an adult before I remember hearing my dad say that he loved me, and then it seemed always to have been a response to my saying it to him. So when I married I wanted to have a son and deeply desired to be the best possible father to him. I yearned for that relationship with him which my dad and I had not been able to have. I bought the football three years too early. I got everything too quickly, because I wanted to make it happen rather than letting it happen. By the time my son was three or four years of age, the same terrible wall was building between us that had come between Daddy and me. I'd say to him, "I love you, son," and any time he did not say it back to me, it hurt me deeply because I already had a deep sense of rejection in me. I wanted so much to know that my son loved me in a way that I was not able to love my father, and my father had not seemed to be able to love me. It's not always a natural response for a three or four-year-old boy to say, "I love you, Daddy" every time you say it to him. But every time my expression of love was missed or ignored, it reminded me of the silence of daddy never saying, "I love you." My son's saying and doing nothing became the trigger, for an agony that reverberated throughout my being. Because neither of us understood why, the problem was compounded. I began to react more and more to my son, and the things he did became too important in both directions. My reaction created a barrier and built walls between us. Our relationship became more and more like mine and daddy's and we never understood why.

I hardly ever got really angry at anyone else. Seldom was I very impatient with others. When it did happen, it was usually my daughter or wife, and most of the time I could trace it back to the fact that I was already upset with my son. It wasn't directly attributable to what my son had done, but rather to what had built up inside of me over a period of many years. He simply triggered what was already festering within my subconscious.

## *Emotional Causes of Rebellion*

Another example of a reaction from the chart would be the matter of "rebellion." In talking to a teenager who was very rebellious I explained the process that had brought her to that point with her parents. One who is rebellious is a person who is angry inside over a sense of rejection from one or both parents. When that anger remains for any length of time it will usually develop into resentment. Likewise, resentment will eventually develop into bitterness. So I said to her, "First of all you became angry at your parents, and after that anger had simmered and stewed inside of you it developed into resentment (resentment is simply anger turning sour). The resentment gradually fermented into bitterness, and rebellion was the inevitable result."

We talked about the fact that the Bible says rebellion is like witchcraft. Now what does that mean? There are many interpretations that could be given to it, but in this application, it means that, like witchcraft, rebellion is selling out to the adversary, the devil. It's giving one's self over to Satan's control. When we allow rebellion to go unchecked, it permits the adversary to develop a stronghold in our life at that point. We gradually lose our willful control in that area. It becomes a spiritual and emotional stronghold which can compulsively control us. The Bible says a stronghold has to be pulled down by God's mighty power (II Corinthians 10:3-5). "This is what has happened in your life," I said to the teenager. "To set you free we must pull that stronghold down."

## *Rejection is the Root*

Let's look more closely at what caused the anger. The chart contends that the root of all emotional hurt related to people is rejection. Rejection is something everyone experiences. Nobody can go through life without experiencing rejection, but some experience more than others. Our basic personality temperament influences how much rejection we experience. One who by temperament is more sensitive emotionally is going to perceive more rejection in the same experience than someone who is not that sensitive. So it's not simply a matter of what we experience. There are several basic factors (personality temperament, sin nature, early environment, religious training, and emotional hurts) which contribute to it. The earlier and more severely we experience rejection, the stronger hold it will tend to have on our lives and the more problems it will cause for us in later years.

## *The Fear of Rejection*

As we begin to have a sense of rejection it will phase into the next item on the chart which is "Fear of Rejection" (by rejection I mean any situation where we're not receiving the love, acceptance, approval or affirmation we need when we need it, in the way we need it, and from whom we need it). As fear of rejection develops, two things happen: (1) We begin to look for it, to anticipate and expect it. Then an immutable law of life comes into play — when we look for anything we always find more of it. This is so, whether we're looking for the good, the bad, or anything else in life. Thus, we begin to sense even more rejection than we're actually receiving, because we are becoming overly sensitive to it (at this point there is always some degree of exaggeration that comes into play). (2) We start building emotional insulation into our lives by putting up emotional defenses, or walls, so we won't be hurt more. Nobody wants to hurt. We are becoming emotionally "gun shy," and don't want to be caught off guard. We don't want to be hurt again by rejection.

## Feeling Becomes Fact

The more we feel we are being rejected, the more we build walls and fences to insulate ourselves against hurt. We build the walls to protect ourselves, to keep from being hurt so much. That's self-survival and it's a very basic instinct, both emotionally and physically. As we develop a fear of rejection, it leads into the third phase, which is a sense of self-rejection. At some point there begins to develop that question within our mind, "Is there something wrong with me? The people that ought to love me the most don't seem to love me as much as I need. Why don't my folks seem to love as much as Billy's or Mary's do them?" We don't know what's going on in Billy's home or Mary's home, but the pasture always looks greener on the other side of the fence, doesn't it? Other times the individual is really being rejected. There is a great deal of child abuse in our nation. We're becoming much more aware of that today. But always the rejection exaggerates our perspective. After a point it doesn't matter how real the rejection is physically; if we perceive it as real, it's going to have the same impact and effect. Where the emotions are concerned, FEELING IS FACT!

## Self-Rejection Develops

The tendency toward self-rejection continues. The feeling grows that "There must be something wrong with me. I am not as lovable, I'm not as likeable, I can't get along with people as easily. A lot of it must be in me." As this develops and solidifies emotionally, it really takes hold in one's life and the result is an increasingly low self-image. Most, if not all people, go through this to some degree growing up, but it's very minimal with some people. With other people it's very strong. Low self-image is a universal problem. I believe that everyone suffers from it to some degree, many simply build a facade through the power of positive thinking and aggressive action. The person who is anger-prone by personality temperament will be more motivated to succeed and "show" people that they are good and worthy. But their surface action seldom really changes what's deep down inside.

Fear will cause us to be less aggressive and less competitive. It will cause us to withdraw and/or give up on ourselves. It allows others to "use" us, and to "walk" on us. This will eventually create an attitude of anger in most people. Anger at others for using us, as well as anger at ourselves for allowing it.

## Anger in Three Directions

When this buildup of rejection comes to the place of creating a low self-image, the two basic emotions of anger and fear are moving to the "reaction level." In those areas where we feel rejected we will be reacting more and responding less. When we became angry on a reaction level our anger is in three directions. First, we are angry at those people by whom we felt rejected — those whom we needed to love us more, or at least communicate it better. Since this invariably begins with parents and siblings it can create deep hurts. All the rationalization and adult understanding in the world will not completely remove it. As a baby or small child we need lots of physical and emotional love and affection. It is the only way a little baby can receive love. You can't write them a letter and tell them how much you love them. You can't go out in the front yard and shout to the neighbors "I love my child — praise God we have a baby!" It doesn't mean a thing to them. They've got to be held, kissed, hugged and loved. They must be played with, and have time and attention from us. When we do not receive it early in life, a seed of anger begins to grow in us over the rejection we feel inside. This anger eventually becomes directed at those by whom we feel rejected.

Second, we get angry at ourselves. The key people who reject us are very important to us, and because we sometimes have very strong anger and even hatred towards them in certain areas, we feel guilty (and I believe that the essence of guilt is anger turned inward). We get mad at ourselves for feeling the way we do toward them. After all, it's "not right" to feel hatred toward one's mother, father, brother or sister, so we must be bad.

Third, we are also angry at God. We feel as though we've been shortchanged. Most people don't consciously blame God that they have these hurts or that they have a low self-image, but deep down they cry out, "If Jesus loved me, he would not let me hurt like this! God, if you really cared you would do something to help me! At least you would let me understand it so I could deal with it, and cope with it." How intense that feeling is depends on how deep the hurt is, and how deep the sense of rejection. One of the most crucial steps in inner healing is to bring the person, particularly Christian, to a realization that he is mad at God. Most of our preaching and teaching has made it so unforgivable to get angry with God that Christians are afraid to face it

## *Guilt is Not of God*

We've had so much bondage preaching that pounds people into the ground. There certainly are negatives in the Bible, and God does hold us accountable and judgment is real. But guilt is of the devil; it's not of God! God convicts through his Holy Spirit, and the purpose of that conviction is to show us we have a need. He wants to help us by bringing us to a point of confessing and releasing that need, so it won't continue to distort our life and create problems for us. He never seeks to put us down, but always to lift us up. Everything He does is for our positive good.

## *Fearful in Three Directions*

Fear progresses in much the same pattern as we have been describing with anger. When it builds to a reaction level, we also become fearful in three directions. We're afraid that those who have been rejecting us will continue to do so. We are also afraid that if we establish new significant relationships, those persons will reject us (this is especially so in divorce and remarriage). In addition, we are afraid that the God who hasn't seemed to care enough to bail us out so far won't do it in the future either.

When the problem of fear relates specifically to our fathers, it compounds our problems with God. Our earthly father is the prototype of the heavenly father. As a child is taught about God the Father, he almost invariably relates Him to what his daddy is like. That can create all kinds of problems in accurately perceiving how much God loves us.

## *Haunted By a Fear*

When ministering to a certain man, God told me one of the things that had haunted that man was the saying, "Like father, like son. Like father, like son." Well, this particular man didn't really have a father. His father abandoned him before he was born. He deserted the man's mother while she was still pregnant. He had one father after another, anybody who would take him in. About the only image he had of a father was someone who didn't care, or who was angry and cruel. It has haunted him all of his life. God revealed this to me in a word of knowledge. As I shared what God had just told me, the tears welled up in his eyes. I said, "God wanted me to tell you some thing else. He said to tell you it's true, like father, like son; like father, like son. But He wants you to remember who your father is. Your father is your heavenly Father. You belong to Him now. He's your daddy! Like father, like son. Like father, like son." What healing took place as God began to release him from a life-long dread. Many people are bound by hurts and fears like that and some go to their graves never having been set free to experience how good life can be!

The root of all that binds us is rejection. The fear of rejection grows out of that. This produces self-rejection and a low self-image, and anger and fear move to the reaction level. Let's look at the chart and the box of Fear Prone tendencies. When someone comes to me who is very shy or introverted it almost always indicates that he or she is a fear-prone person. Fear is what causes a person to be overly shy (I am not referring here to an inner quietness which is quite a different thing). A person who is very shy is insecure. Often the person is basically sad inside. Frequently they are depression-prone though depression can grow out of anger as well as fear. Many times they are people who have deep sense of loneliness and hopelessness. They need to come to understand that this, too, grows out of their fear which is rooted in the fear of rejection. They are afraid that people are not going to like them and may not approve of them. How many times have you had the feeling, "If people really knew me they wouldn't like me"? That's the fear of rejection we have because of the deep-seated feeling that no one really loves us unconditionally. The only person that can completely love us with no strings attached is Jesus. But if we're angry at God because we feel we've been short-changed, and/or we're afraid of Him we simply cannot believe that He loves us unconditionally. Our concept of Him and of ourselves prevents it to any great degree. So few Christians really know how unconditional His love is.

## *Jesus Loves Unconditionally*

Through inner healing Jesus heals a person where he hurts most, and as He does the person begins to realize how much God does love him. He loves us just as we are — loves and accepts us without having to approve of everything about us! What a revelation to understand that. If we never got any better, if we were never any different, God would still love us just as much. In John 17:23 Jesus is talking to the Father. He is in the Garden of Gethsemane the night before the crucifixion. This is the real Lord's Prayer, where Jesus said, "Father, somehow let my disciples (my followers) know that you love them as much as you love me" (Eargle Paraphrase).

I remember when I discovered that verse in 1971 and what it did for me. I remember what I wrote in the margin of my Bible. The first time I read it I wrote "Ohh!" After reading it a second time I wrote, "WOW!" And I still get chill bumps when I think about it. It is still soaking in — that Jesus loves me that much. He loves you that much. He loves us more than we'll ever realize, but what a wonderful growing "knowing" it is to have in us.

Now look at the chart again. Everyone has both fear and anger in them, but when those emotions develop to a reaction level, there's usually a stronger tendency to go in one direction or the other. Let's say a person might be 65% anger-prone and 35% fear-prone, as an example; it could be any kind of mix. And sometimes there's enough of both in a person that he fluctuates back and forth between the two.

## A Difference in Anger

Notice the Anger box. If anger grows in a person to the point of resentment and bitterness, and continues until it reaches the level of violence, that anger will be expressed against other people and/or other people's property. For example, those who commit vandalism are people who are angry inside. Usually they have strong anger towards those in authority. When they vandalize a church building, they are angry toward God and those in authority.

On the other hand, when a fear-prone person moves to the point of violence, it will more likely be self-violence, even suicide. The fear-prone person is the one who is most likely to take his own life; the anger-prone person is more likely to harm, or take the life of someone else.

## Over Concern with Symptoms

One of the most important things God has taught me through using this chart is never to become overly concerned with symptoms. If someone comes to me who is addicted to hard drugs, I don't spend much time talking with him about drugs. The use of drugs is only a symptom, or surface problem. Alcoholism is a symptom. Homosexuality is a symptom. That which we see on the surface is basically only symptomatic of the real problem which is rooted in the subconscious. As the hurts are healed in the power of Christ, the symptoms will usually begin to disappear.

A common example of this would be bed-wetting. We've counseled a number of people who have had bed-wetting problems. Most did not come simply because of the bed-wetting, although that can be an acute problem, particularly as one gets older. Numerous adults still have this problem. Imagine, if you can, the embarrassment and humiliation that can come from it in the adult years. A young woman came with this problem. She told me in the third session that she had had a bed-wetting problem all of her life, but that she hadn't had it since the first session. Whatever it was that caused it, Jesus had healed it in our first session together. This has happened repeatedly with children, teenagers and adults, but we never dealt with the symptom. Many times they couldn't even talk about the symptom. They were too embarrassed by it. God takes us to where the hurts are and heals those hurts, and the symptoms that are an outgrowth of those hurts are removed as a result.

## More Negative Emotions

Now let's move to the third box on the chart. It is the elongated one below the fear and anger boxes. This is a box of negative emotional characteristics that can grow out of either anger or fear. Worry, tension, nervousness, frustration, depression, irresponsibility, self-deception, confusion, forgetfulness, exaggeration, frigidity, impotence, sexual lust, jealousy, manipulation, lying, guilt — and many others. They are negative characteristics which fear and anger produce in our lives.

## *The Progression of Depression*

The box at the bottom of the page is an explanation of what I call simple or common depression. The kind of depression that most of us see 90% of the time begins with a specific disappointment or experience or rejection. When a person who is depressed comes to me, I frequently ask him a simple question: "How long have you felt depressed?" If he says, "three months," I might reply, "Tell me what happened that really disappointed you about three or three and a half months ago." Most of the time God brings to mind the specific hurting memory which triggered the depression. We do inner healing for the memory and the surface depression is frequently broken in the first session. The additional inner healing is required to heal the other significant hurts which have caused him to be depression-prone .

This box on depression also illustrates that if we do not know how to properly deal with our disappointments, they can lead us into discouragement. If we are depression-prone, this discouragement can continue on into despondency and despair. In addition, the box shows that depression not only always involves self-pity, but that the self-pity grows stronger as the depression becomes deeper. They feed each other in a self-propelling cycle. The earlier the cycle of depression is caught the easier it is to heal. The process of inner healing almost always requires the willingness of the individual. They must desire for the depression to be broken, because God will not usurp their free will.

Ultimately there is only one medication that can heal every negative emotion and hurt listed on this chart. It is the medicine of Jesus' love. That's what inner healing is all about. It is an especially anointed tool of God for applying his unconditional love in those hard-to-get-at place in the deep recesses of our being. And it works!

## *Two Kinds of Hurts*

Imagine, if you will, that the emotional hurts inside of you are like a "house of hurts." Every house has two kinds of walls. There are partition walls and load-bearing walls. Partition walls simply divide a house into rooms. Load-bearing walls not only divide a house into rooms, but they also help to support the structure of the house, holding it together.

You can remove every partition wall and all you will get are larger rooms. However, when you remove the load-bearing walls, you are affecting the basic structure of the house. The roof will begin to sag, the walls to lean inward, and eventually, the entire house can collapse.

It is the same way with our emotional house of hurts. We have two kinds of hurts: partition and load-bearing. An adult with a strong sense of rejection may have several thousand partition (or less significant) hurts inside. To understand and deal with each one could indeed take years, but out of all those hurts only a few dozen will be deeply significant, or load-bearing.

The load-bearing hurts are the ones which hold our house of hurts together, and that must be torn down. These are the ones we must let God show us and heal. As this is done, each load-bearing hurt which is pulled down takes all the partition hurts with it which tie into it. Thus the basic structure of the house is being altered with the healing of each hurting memory. This is the only healing of the memories that is absolutely essential to our emotional balance and wholeness.

## *Three Steps to Inner Healing*

God has shown me a three-step process to use in the healing of the memory of these load-bearing hurts. The healing formula involves confession, forgiveness and prayer.

## *Confess Your Wrong Reactions*

First, we must learn the imperative confession. We must confess the wrong reactions that we've had toward those who've hurt us — not wrong because they are unjustified, necessarily, but because they are wrong for us. They are bad for us — self-defeating and counter-productive. Wrong because God loves us and does not want us to hurt. Wrong because many times we are in actuality punishing ourselves for what someone else did to us, even years ago. This makes no sense and is not good for anyone — us or them. It is self-destructive (for further explanation, request Teaching 128 entitled, "How To Respond, Rather Than React"). The biblical word that is translated "confess' in the New Testament means to "agree with God;" we agree that what He is saying to us is right. To do this authentically, we also repent because we stop alibiing and blaming others and line up with what God is saying on the subject. This allows us to experience God's forgiveness (1 John 1:9-10). When we confess He automatically forgives and His forgiveness works as a spiritual antiseptic to cleanse our emotional wound.

## *Forgive Those Who've Hurt You*

Next we must forgive the person(s) who has hurt us — not necessarily because we feel like it, but because it's right. Right because God's Word says to forgive and right for both us and them. It is an act of the will, not an emotional feeling. Unwillingness to forgive will short-circuit the entire inner healing process (this also includes forgiving ourselves, which for many is the hardest aspect). Many times we are unwilling to forgive someone who has hurt us because we do not feel they deserve it. When this is the case, we forgive them because we deserve it! We don't deserve to hurt any more for what someone else did to us, perhaps years ago. We deserve to be set free in Christ by forgiving. He wants you free so He can use you to free others.

## *Remove it with Prayer Visioning*

In the most significant hurts, a third step is frequently required to remove the backlog of hurt and sting. We must completely forget it through prayer visioning. We must allow Jesus to come in through prayer visioning and completely remove it "as far as the East is from the West." Humanly speaking, we have relatively little ability to forget, to actually remove a memory (not simply bury it in our subconscious). But spiritually, through prayer visioning, Jesus can totally remove the hurt associated with the painful experience. When this is properly done, all hurting aspects of the memory should be gone forever, as with my fear of heights and falling described in Chapter 1.

## *The Story of Billy*

Let me tell you a story to illustrate these first two important steps of confession and forgiveness. It was night, and two-year-old Billy was asleep in his bed. His daddy came home drunk in the middle of the night. Stumbling through the darkened house, he knocked over a lamp with a loud crash. The noise awakened Billy and he began to cry. His drunken father made his way to the door of Billy's room and shouted, "Shut up, kid, and go back to sleep!" The startled, half-asleep child cried even more. The furious father staggered across to Billy's bed and began spanking him hard. The terrified, disoriented child began to scream, and his dad flipped out into a fit of rage. Hitting and beating the boy, he finally picked him up and threw him against the wall.

Billy was in the hospital recuperating for nearly a month from the beating. His first two emotional responses were hurt and fear. It was not long, however, until he began to experience some others — anger and resentment. He was mad that he had been treated this way by his father. In time, out of the anger and resentment grew bitterness and rebellion. Billy was badly treated by his father several more times over the years, and there was never a real closeness, affection nor love between them.

## Dad Begins to Change

As he neared his teen years his dad accepted Christ, stopped drinking, and tried to change. He really worked at being a good father and making amends, but as Billy grew older he still found himself rebelling against his dad's authority. He didn't understand why, and neither did his father. They both knew that he had really changed — but the hurt and anger from childhood was still there, festering in the sub-conscious. They continued to grow apart through his teen years and, upon finishing high school, Billy left home. At twenty he married. In the next few years he had two children. His dad died when Billy was twenty-eight, and at thirty he came to see me, nearly bursting inside emotionally. He found himself reacting in anger more and more to his wife and children, particularly to his son.

Billy and I talked about inner healing, and I explained to him that it revolves around the healing of the memories of the load-bearing hurts in one's life. The experience when he was two years old was certainly one of those significant hurts. I explained to Billy about the three basic steps in Inner healing — confession, forgiveness and prayer visioning. "The first thing you must do to receive healing of that hurt, Billy, is to confess your wrong reactions toward your dad for what he did to you." He reacted to my statement by saying, "Me, confess! Are you crazy? My old man beats me up when I'm two years old, I'm in the hospital for a month, and you tell me to confess! You have to be crazy! If you want somebody to confess, talk to my old man, not me!"

When he had finished reacting, I explained to Billy what I mean by a "wrong reaction." It was not wrong because his feelings were unjustified. The hurt, fear and anger were very justified. Probably no one could have experienced what he had at two years of age and not have been angry and resentful. It was totally justified. Neither was it wrong because he was to blame. In that particular experience his daddy was probably 100% at fault. So what did I mean by wrong reactions?

## Why was it Wrong

His reaction was wrong, because it was wrong for him, "Billy, God loves you, and He doesn't want you to hurt. He wants you to have a full and abundant life, and you can't with anger, resentment and bitterness inside of you. It hurts you and distorts your perspective and causes you to hurt others. Look at how you are reacting to your wife and children. You are actually punishing yourself and them for what your daddy did to you twenty-eight years ago! That's completely wrong! It's senseless and self-defeating. That's what I mean by a wrong reaction."

## *Agree with God*

"In the New Testament, the word 'confess' means 'to agree with God that what he is saying to you is right.' So, Billy, the first step in allowing God to heal this hurt and remove it once and for all is to agree with God that you have had that anger and resentment toward your dad all these years. Then acknowledge that it's wrong for you, that you are deeply sorry for it and that you don't want it anymore. This releases it to Him, and His forgiveness comes flowing into you to cleanse away all the infection from that hurt" (1 John 1:9).

"Only then are you ready to take the second step in inner healing. Now, for the first time you are ready to forgive your father." Until we confess we cannot receive forgiveness, and until we receive it, we don't have any to pass along to someone else in a load-bearing hurt situation (trying to forgive without confessing is why we so often can't forget the hurt). When we have difficulty forgiving someone, it is because we have a problem at one of three points: (1) We don't feel like it, or (2) we don't feel like they deserve it, or (3) we still want to get back at the one who has hurt us.

## **REMOVING BARRIERS TO FORGIVING**

"Billy, let me explain these three areas. First, you don't have to have any strong emotional feeling to be able to forgive. We don't do it because of feelings, but because it's right. It's right not only because God's Word says so, but also, because it's right for us (if we don't forgive them, our forgiveness becomes a block to God forgiving us, just like the anger and resentment were). Secondly, we don't have to forgive someone who has hurt us because they deserve it. They may or may not, but God has never forgiven us on that basis, and neither are we compelled to do so. He forgives us because it is His nature and is right for Him whether we receive it or not. For example, Jesus' death on the cross. We are to forgive because it is right and because we are to be like Jesus, but also, because we do not deserve to go on hurting for what someone else has done to us.

"Billy, you do not deserve to go on hurting for what your daddy did to you twenty-eight years ago, but you must forgive him to set yourself free. Understanding this is so important. Third, we must not let any desire for revenge keep us from being set free (just confess it like the anger). Most Christians never make any real effort to get back at a person anyway. We just think about it occasionally, and let the devil have another means to hurt us. Billy, you have been gone from home for twelve years, and your dad has been dead for two, so how can you possibly get back at him?"

## *Dumb, But Not Stupid*

"When I finally understood these things in my own life, God showed me that not to confess and forgive would not only be dumb, but it would be stupid (dumb is when we don't know better. Stupid is when we know better, but don't do anything about it). All of us are dumb in some areas, but I was determined that I did not want to be stupid, now that I knew better! Billy, if you will take these two steps God will set you free of this hurt. If there is any hurt or sting left, then we will go to God in prayer visioning and let Jesus complete the healing once and forever. He loves you and wants to heal all your hurts, and meet all of your needs" (Philippians 4:19).

## *What Jesus Did*

Let me give you a typical testimony which I hear over and over again as I get back with people, after we've done inner healing. We've healed certain experiences in one session, and the next session I will frequently begin by saying, "Okay, let's look at the experiences that God healed in the last session. What practical benefits and changes have you actually seen over this last week from those experiences we healed?" The reply will be something like this: "It doesn't bother me any more" Then they will frequently say, "Do you know what the most beautiful part is? I especially remember what Jesus did, when He came in and healed it." Over and over again people say, "What I remember is what Jesus did when He came in and He loved me and He healed that hurt and took it away." The hurt and sting are gone! It's not there any more. And the memory that one is so frequently going to have is of what Jesus did.

We talk about falling in love with Jesus. Prayer visioning makes us fall in love with Him. I've had many people tell me, "You know I'm appreciative for what you have done, and how you have helped me, and how God has used you, but it's not you that I really appreciate. It's not you that I give the glory to, its Jesus, because

Jesus is the one who healed me." No one in the world can heal. No doctor has ever lived that can heal. No minister or counselor has ever lived that can heal. Only God can heal, and God heals through Jesus!

## *A Healing Prayer*

Father, I know that I've covered a lot in this chapter, and that some who read it are going to have to really wrestle with it. It will take time for all of it to register with them. Others have already been convicted of hurts and needs in their own life and want to be set free. I thank you that you want us to be healed and whole — physically, emotionally and spiritually — and the most basic level is spiritual.

So, Father, for everyone who is reaching out to you now, I pray that that the work of your Holy Spirit might bring them to the realization that the deepest need in their life is to come to know Jesus Christ as their personal Lord and Savior. That this is the beginning point for everything else. Then, help them to see that it is just the beginning point-

By your Spirit, create openness and responsiveness in the life of each one who reads these words, that they might begin to know not only that they hurt (because it's important that we come to that realization and face up to it), but, Oh, Father, that they might come to know that here is hope for the healing of their hurt in Jesus. That you don't want them to hurt. That you want to heal them of every hurt in their life. That you want to meet every need that exists in their being, and that you want to minister to them with your love. Let them know that you love them — love them with your agape love that has no strings attached.

Thank you, Father. Amen.

# The ROOT of REJECTION
## FEAR of REJECTION
## SELF-REJECTION
## LOW SELF-IMAGE

(EVERYONE HAS BOTH FEAR AND ANGER, BUT ONE IS ALWAYS A STRONGER PERSONALITY FACTOR)

**FEAR Tendency**
(Some characteristics of fear prone people)

| | |
|---|---|
| Shyness | Inadequacy |
| Introverted | Clumsiness |
| Insecurity | Negativism |
| Sadness | Doubt |
| Loneliness | Perplexity |
| Hopelessness | Indecision |
| Laxiness | Superstition |
| Fantasy | Self-Violence |
| Daydreaming | Suicide |
| Escapism | Self-Condemnation |
| Perfectionism | Masochism |
| Anxiety, Dread | Fear of Failure |
| Worry | Financial Fear |
| Moody | Fear of People |
| Embarassment | (Men, women, |
| Over-Sensitive | children or |
| Self-Pity | peers) |
| Phobias | Fear of |
| Persecution | Confrontation |
| Hysteria | |
| Inferiority | |

**NO ONE HAS ALL THE CHARACTERISTICS IN EITHER BOX. THEY ARE SIMPLY INDICATIVE OF THE TYPES OF SECONDARY REACTIONS THAT GROW OUT OF ANGER AND FEAR**

**ANGER Tendency**
(Some characteristics of anger prone people)

| | |
|---|---|
| Resentment | Egotistical |
| Bitterness | Self-Righteous |
| Cruel | Self-Sufficient |
| Sarcastic | Inconsiderate |
| Teasing | Intolerance |
| Revengeful | Irritability |
| Rage | Impatience |
| Hatred | Aggressiveness |
| Violence | Confrontation |
| Hostility | Restlessness |
| Critical | Pouting |
| Argumentative | Intemperance |
| Cursing | Sadism |
| Dominating | Overly |
| Unforgiving | Competitive |
| Compulsive | Hostility |
| Disobedient | towad People |
| Stubborn | (Men, women, |
| Rebellious | children or |
| Proud | peers) |
| Selfish | |

**COMMON TO BOTH ANGER AND FEAR**

| | | | | | |
|---|---|---|---|---|---|
| Tension | Self-Deception | Forgetfulness | Jealousy | Lying | |
| Nervousness | Confusion | Exaggeration | Possessivenes | Guilt | |
| Frustration | Greed | Frigidity | Overeating | Mental Illness | |
| Depression | Fatigue | Impotence | Addictions | Insomnia | |
| Gossip | Sleeplessness | Sexual Lust | Ambivalence | Sickness | |
| Irresponsibility | Psychosomatic | Masturbation | Manipulation | Self-pity | |

**THE BEGINNING AND PROGRESSION OF "COMMON" DEPRESSION**

**DISAPPOINTMENT**
1. DISCOURAGEMENT (SELF-PITY)
2. DESPONDENCY (SELF-PITY-Y)
3. DESPAIR (SELF-PITY-Y-Y)
4. CATATONIC STATE

*This chart is not designed to be used or properly understood apart from the teaching sessions by the author.*

## Inner Healing Reactions Chart

This chart does not deal with NORMAL EMOTIONAL RESPONSES to a given situation, but rather with ABNORMAL REACTIONS, (or Over-Reactions), where the immediate situation simply TRIGGERS A REACTION from within our sub-conscious. The response then is DISPROPORTIONATE to what is happening. There is too much anger, fear, etc. WE OVER-REACT.

The EMOTIONAL ROOT of many such reactions is REJECTION. Continuing experiences of rejection often will creat a SENSE OF REJECTION. This sense of rejection may develop at any point from the fetus to the recent past. When it does, and as it continues to grow in its grip on our emotional life we will begin to develop a FEAR OF REJECTION. This, then, distorts our perspective causing us to feel more rejection than we're actually experiencing. So we begin to become more cautious with and suspicious of others, and to create protective emotional walls to insulate ourselves from additional hur and rejection. This will eventually lead to SELF-REJECTION and consequently A LOW SELF-IMAGE.

As these processes develop within us emotionally they increase the tendency to bury the memory of these hurts, and to make ourselves forget them. The solution is not to be found in the treating of the surface symptoms, but in understanding the root cause of our problems and allowing God to do inner healing.

This Inner healing often requires the HEALING OF MEMORIES so that we can be set free again to Respond, rather than to React. The chart (with proper explanation and application) is designed to facilitate this. It is a tool for allowing Jesus to show us where the significant hurts are and to aid us in walking back into those hurting memories with him so that He can heal them. It is also designed to show us that our emotions follow a logical progression, and when properly understood are predictable and preventable. They are not a hodge-podge of confusion, but the product of a cause and result relationship which is more intricate than complex.

(Continued from Previous Page)

---

Copyright 2019. JON EARGLE MINISTRIES, INC., Knoxville, TN
All Rights Reserved. International Copyright Secured.

*Chapter 3*

# OVERCOMING ANGER, RESENTMENT, AND BITTERNESS

Do you ever lose your cool? Ever become more angry than you should? Do you periodically realize that certain things are still eating at you inside? Have you tried to forgive certain people for what they did to you, but found that you can't seem to forget? If so, it may well indicate that you have a problem with repressed anger.

## *EVERYONE GETS ANGRY*

If that's the case, don't take a guilt trip. You are in good company, for everyone gets angry. There are no exceptions. Everyone gets angry sometimes, even the ones who you think do not. They do. This includes those people who seem so cool, calm and collected on the surface. Anger just shows more with some people, and it is more frequent with some than others. Its intensity can vary tremendously. If you measure it on a scale of one to one hundred, someone might have anger on a scale of twenty and another might measure a ninety-five. There is a great deal of difference in the intensity, but both are angry. It's only a matter of degree. One of the things that is so important for us to realize is that everything is this way — it is a matter of degree. You know, it's not a matter that a Christian either walks in the Spirit, or he does not. If he is a born again child of God, he must walk in the Spirit to some degree. It's not a matter of whether he does or he doesn't; it is to what degree he does. To be filled with the Spirit means to be controlled by the Spirit, and out of that control grows his power. Every born again believer is letting Christ control him or her to some degree, but for one it may only be a 3% degree, and for somebody else it might be 93%, so it's a matter of degree. It's the same with anger. We all have it; it's simply a matter of degree. It is important for us to learn how to handle it properly to keep from hurting ourselves, and others.

### *Response or Reaction Level*

This anger which is inside of us can be on a response or a reaction level. We discussed the difference between these two in the previous chapter, but let's review very briefly. When we react in anger, it is just the opposite. It is greater than the situation warrants and difficult to get under control. We frequently just end up pushing it back down inside and slapping on the lid. Then it simply starts building again. It is important for us to understand the difference between responding and reacting. We should be able to identify when we are responding and when we are reacting, as well as when someone else is. To be able to do so can help save a friendship, or a business deal, and even our witness for Christ, because, as we said in Chapter 2, we don't have to take a reaction personally when we properly understand it. The person is that upset, but not that upset merely at us.

## ANGER IS NOT ALWAYS WRONG

It is also essential for us to realize that anger is not always automatically wrong. This is important. Anger is not always wrong. Does that startle you? Most of the time in our churches, we've been taught that it is always wrong, with the possible exception of what we refer to as "righteous indignation," as the time when Jesus went into the Temple, saw the money changers and chased them out with a whip. Righteous indignation is okay when we have it, but we're not quite sure what it is, or whether we ever really have it. We know it's not what we get most of the time, because there isn't much righteousness in the anger most of us have. So we tend to think that anger is always wrong, but it's not.

The Bible says, "Be angry and sin not" (Ephesians 4:26A). It is not saying, "Don't ever be angry," but is saying 'Be angry without letting it become sin." This must mean it is possible to be angry without sinning. It also says, "Let lot the sun do down on your anger (or wrath)" (Ephesians 4:26B). There is a difference between temptation and sin, and this is so in every area. Anger is not wrong when it is temptation, before it becomes sin. When we are simply tempted to be angry, we know that is not sin. Martin Luther said concerning temptation, "You may not be able ;o keep the birds from flying over your head, but you can are vent them from building a nest in your hair." We may lot be able to keep anger from coming initially to mind, 3ut we can keep it from nesting and building a home, taking up residence. The problem of anger is not so much .with the initial feeling of anger as it is with the attitude of anger. That feeling may be allowable, but the attitude is lot. To put it another way — anger is okay on a response level, but it is wrong on a reaction level.

### *What's Really Wrong*

The thing that is most wrong is not in having anger, but in not dealing with that anger in the right way. It is important that we understand the difference between suppress and repress. Psychologically, to suppress something means to control it; to repress something means to bury it. One of the things we must learn how to do is to control our anger, but not control it by burying it down inside of us. This control ultimately comes out of being able to release t, rather than repressing it within our subconscious, and being deceived into thinking that we've "forgotten" it. We release it through confession and forgiveness.

## SYMPTOMS OF ANGER

We'll expand on that a little later, but first let's look at some of the symptoms of an angry person as shown on The Reactions Chart. We need to be able to recognize anger. Many people don't unless they see someone with their fist doubled up and drawn back, or someone who is all red in the face. There are people like that, but anger is usually much more subtle. What are some of the symptoms of an angry person that we can begin to recognize? The most basic symptom is resentment. One cannot have anger buried down inside for any length of time without its growing into resentment. Resentment is simply anger turning sour and resentment continuing to sour produces bitterness. It takes some time to learn how to identify the difference with preciseness, but it's important that we learn that we are talking about degrees and expressions of anger. Anger produces resentment, which in turn breeds bitterness. Those three things stewing down inside of us can cause all kinds of problems from migraine headaches and stomach ulcers to backaches and arthritis, to almost anything that we want to name in a wide variety of physical ailments, as well as emotional ones. I am not saying that every time we have a headache, or an ulcer, or arthritis it's from that, but I am saying that even medically we know that these are primary causes of many problems. Doctors are saying more and more that perhaps the primary cause of heart-related problems is stress. Stress comes from not understanding and dealing with our emotions, repressing rather than releasing the hurts inside.

### *Rebellion Develops*

When anger, resentment, and bitterness are present, they will inevitably produce rebellion. Rebellion grows out of anger and resentment at feeling rejected by those who have authority over us. Rebellion grows where anger and resentment are already present. People who are rebellious think they are doing their own thing, but they are not. They are doing what their emotions are compelling them to do, because they are controlled by what is inside of them. So, not only do resentment and bitterness grow out of anger, but rebellion and disobedience do also. All these grow out of anger, and anger is always rooted in rejection. Understanding rejection is the key to everything emotionally.

A man came to my office one day who epitomized this rebellion growing out of rejection. Anger was etched in his face. He had come because his wife had dared him, telling him he was too cowardly to do so. He had recently separated from her and was preparing to file for divorce. Anger was so strong in him that on several occasions he had nearly killed someone. This deep anger to the point of rage was rooted in childhood rebellion toward his parents — his dad had been an alcoholic and his mother was dominating and a "nagger."

Rebellion, rooted in his sense of rejection from them, had locked in and steadily grown since the day his dad shot his dog — his once close companion. From that time on he became increasingly rebellious toward both man and God. Not long after, he had chased his father with a butcher knife and twice nearly killed fellow soldiers while in the military.

But underneath was a real gentleness and a deep need to know that he was loved — that someone cared. As Jesus began to love him and heal his emotional wounds, the rage began to dissipate, much of the rebellion disappeared and the one who was totally rejected began to take his rejection upon Himself. Little by little he began to see that there is One who really cares and loves us unconditionally.

## *Anger Produces Impatience*

Impatience also grows out of anger. I remember when God told me this, and I thought he was mistaken. I said, "No, God, you're wrong!" (Have you ever told God he is wrong? It's not very smart, but that's what I used to do.) I said, "God, I've taken quite a few psychology courses and you don't understand. Impatience doesn't grow out of anger; anger grows out of impatience. Anybody knows that!" It took me some time to properly understand what He was saying. It's the difference, again, between a response and a reaction. On a normal response level, anger does indeed grow out of impatience. Something is irritating to you, and you gradually become more and more impatient, until it produces anger. Okay? That's on a response level. However, when the anger in a given area has already reached a reaction level, it will first express itself through impatience. You are already subconsciously angry in that area and when anyone provokes you at that point you have no real ability to be patient. If you have problems with impatience, realize that it is very likely evidence of the fact that there is a lot of anger already stored up inside of you. You are angry because you feel rejected in the areas where you are most important.

## *Additional Symptoms*

Additional symptoms of anger are teasing, sarcasm, and an argumentative attitude. All these are evidences, in most cases, of anger inside. When you have a real problem in any of these areas, it is because of repressed anger. They are release valves for our anger. God doesn't show us these things to condemn us, but to set us free from them. He wants us to agree with Him about it so He can show us how to release them. You can't be healed if you don't know you are sick. I have a little card on my desk which says, "If you want to get well, you've got to stop doing what made you sick." How true!

A final symptom worthy of our attention is over-competitiveness — not just competitiveness but over-competitiveness, e.g., the father who has to defeat his son in every game they play. I'm convinced that one of the things that makes many pro-athletes successful is because they have a lot of anger inside of them. Their anger also helps them to cope with the pain that they have from injuries. When we get angry, our pain threshold goes up and we don't feel pain as intensely. When we are fearful, our pain threshold goes down and we feel pain much more readily. The fear-prone person has a more difficult time being successful athletically, unless driven by a fear of failure. One of the reasons why some pro-athletes get into trouble with the law after their athletic careers have ended is because they no longer have a socially acceptable way to release their anger. When they have lost that outlet, the anger is still there. So, simply ventilating the anger isn't the answer, because sooner or later we'll get into a situation where we don't have an acceptable outlet, then it an get us into real trouble. We must learn to deal with it biblically.

## THE PRIMARY CAUSE OF ANGER

A fifth area I want to discuss in this chapter is the primary cause of anger. It is my deep conviction that anger s directly traceable to rejection. In fact, I believe that the root cause of all anger and related problems is rejection. Few people, including most professional counselors, really understand this. The root of ALL emotional hurt is rejection. It doesn't matter what the emotional hurt is or the negative emotion involved. It is ultimately traceable back o an experience of rejection. To understand this, you are probably going to have to expand your understanding of he meaning of the word rejection. It was a word with a very narrow meaning and definition to me a few years ago. Being disappointed by someone is being rejected. Rejection permeates all of life. There is no way to go through life and not experience rejection. There's just no way. The most loving, wonderful parents in the world are going to give heir children some experiences of rejection. It's part of being human. Much rejection is not intentional at all, but t can still be very destructive and devastating to the per-on who is on the receiving end. REJECTION MEANS NOT RECEIVING THE LOVE, ACCEPTANCE, AFFIRMATION OR APPROVAL THAT YOU NEED FROM WHOM YOU NEED IT, WHEN YOU NEED IT, IN THE WAY YOU NEED IT. It can be real or imagined. As we are hurt by others we tend to become more cautious and suspicious distorting our perspective even more. It doesn't mean we're not receiving rejection, but it means no matter what amount of it we are receiving, it is exaggerated to some degree and seems worse than it actually is.

Rejection is often caused not so much by the failure of others to love us, as it is by their failure to communicate that love to us in a way that we can sufficiently relate to, and receive. Most parents, for instance, love their children, but there are relatively few parents who are always successful at communicating it in the way the child needs. So all of us grow up with the feeling at times that we are not really loved. Many children grow up feeling they are loved when they are good, and not loved when they are bad; loved when what they do is approved of by their parents, but not really loved when the parents don't approve.

Anger can grow out of someone else's rejection of our loved ones. It can be direct rejection of us, or it can be a rejection of somebody that is special to us. We may become angry over that! It is still rejection, though indirect rejection.

Do you know what may be the most consistent and frequent form of rejection there is? Rejection of ourselves. Self-rejection. So many people are bound by this throughout their entire lives, along with the guilt and defeat that it produces, making it the primary factor in low self-image.

## *A Review of Rejection*

It is important at this point that we review some of what I said in Chapter 2 about rejection. Everybody experiences rejection. To the degree that we experience rejection, we begin to develop a sense of rejection. As that sense of rejection grows (the sense that we are not getting the love, acceptance, affirmation and approval which we need), to that degree we begin to develop a fear of rejection. We begin to be afraid that we are going to be rejected. As we become afraid of being rejected by people whose love we need and depend on, we begin to be cautious. We start putting up some fences and eventually walls to try to insulate ourselves to keep people from hurting us. We need that love, but there have been too many times when we've reached out, or opened up, and we were rejected. So we [raw back. We start building higher and thicker walls. We ill do this. There is not anyone who doesn't. The only difference is one of degree. The degree of one's fear of rejection relates to a number of things, but the most basic is low strong a sense of rejection we have. Another factor which has not been touched on is our basic personality temperament. We are born with different personality temperaments. There are no two people exactly alike. Different temperaments have different degrees of sensitivity. For example, if a brother and sister are brought up together in basically the same circumstances and one is more sensitive emotionally than the other, that one will perceive more rejection. The rejection will be deeper and more harmful to them than it is to the one who is less sensitive. So it isn't simply a matter of rejection in our environment.

## Basic Influencing Factors

There are five basic factors which cause us to act the way we do. They are the sin nature, our environment, physical health, personality temperament and emotional hurts. The latter two are the ones with which we are most concerned at this point. Our basic temperament determines much of our emotional sensitivity to people and things, which in turn directly effects the degree of rejection we feel in a given experience. The irony is that the most sensitive people also frequently have the greater capacity for love and compassion. When we recoil in rejection, we stifle that compassion out of fear preventing God's love from flowing through us. Two of the most basic instincts and needs that God has built into us are the need to love and be loved. No one is complete without either one. It s giving and receiving. We cannot be balanced, whole persons unless we are both giving and receiving love. To he degree that we have a sense of rejection and fear of rejection, we are not able to open ourselves up and really commit to somebody else. I believe the most basic problem n marital relations is the fear of rejection, and the fear of commitment which grows out of it. One has to let Jesus heal the memory of those hurts inside, from which grow that sense of rejection and consequently the low self-image.

## Failure to Communicate

This rejection can begin anywhere from the fetus, to the recent past. But if we have very many hurts, they have not occurred overnight. A sense of rejection didn't begin last week. It is a slow building process. The earlier we experience rejection and the more of it we experience early in our lives, the stronger the tendency is to have a sense of rejection and thus a fear of rejection. What happens when children experience rejection? They don't know how to understand it, nor how to cope with it. A child does not know why he is being treated that way. A two-year-old doesn't know why he is not being loved. He just knows he is not getting what he needs emotionally. He can only receive love in the simplest, most basic fashion. We can be crazy about him and not communicate it. That especially happens with fathers. The only thing that little boy can understand is our picking him up and loving and hugging him. We can write him three love letters a day and it doesn't mean a thing to him. We can rent the most powerful PA system in the world, go downtown and shout at the top of our lungs how much we love him and it won't mean anything to a little child! This is where we fail so much of the time. Mothers are usually better about it than fathers. There are relatively few men who really know how to express love to small children. Many don't even see their responsibility until their children are old enough to play ball and participate in team sports. Others are unaware of their responsibility until the teenage years. By then they have lost much of their opportunity, because the preschool years are so critical in our personality development. I doubt that it is possible in those first few years to give a child too much love and affection. There may be other times when they get older that it can be embarrassing to them, but a small child must have it to grow up securely. We are building security into them that will stand them in good stead against rejection. If we don't, they will not be able to cope with the hurts and rejection that the world is going to give them.

This generation probably has more pressure than any in history. I thank God that I am not a teenager. I had plenty of temptations, certainly all I could handle, but not what teenagers have today. It seems to get worse with each generation. My dad is in his late seventies, and sometimes I pause to reflect about what has happened technologically in his lifetime. Neither the automobile nor airplane existed when he was born. Radio and television did not. Almost anything that one could name that we take for granted today was not even in existence seventy-seven years ago. The pressure of all this change just keeps on building and building and building like a snowball going downhill. No wonder we have been hurting people.

## *Angry in Three Directions*

It is also important for us to understand that we are angry in three directions. We are angry at ourselves, which is expressed by guilt. We are angry at the people who have rejected us, and we're angry at God. Do you realize that? We're angry at Him because to some degree, we either feel he helped cause our problem, or that He obviously doesn't really care about us, or else he would bail us out of this hurting mess.

*Chapter 3: Overcoming Anger, Resentment, and Bitterness*

## *A Healing Vision*

The final thing that I want to say about anger is that we must deal with it. We must learn how to suppress it and not repress it. We must learn how to control it and release it, without burying it. There are not very many people who really know how to do this. Most people who think they are controlling it are really burying it. All they are doing is talking about surface control while anger is seething down inside of them. I'm talking about real control. To do this we must make the three steps of inner healing part of our permanent emotional and spiritual lifestyle. Let's review them. First, we must Confess Our Wrong Reactions. Second, we must Forgive Those Who Have Hurt Us, and finally, in some instances to forget it completely, we will have to take it to the Lord for Prayer Visioning, and in our spirits see or sense Him healing the memory of any remaining emotional sting. Let me share with you just one experience of God's healing where anger and resentment were released through prayer visioning.

Mary" came for counseling, hurting inside, but not knowing why. When she was twelve years old she had two sisters, one ten and the other four. Her youngest sister was very sickly, weighing only fifteen pounds. Mary had become like a mother to her, taking care of her like she was her little baby. Her life revolved around this little sister who suddenly died, leaving Mary devastated. Mary was standing before a window looking outward — gazing at the heavens. I said, "May I tell you what you are thinking about as you look out the window?" (How did I know what she was thinking? Only because the Spirit of God told me.) She granted me permission and I said, "What you are thinking is 'God, why did you have to do this? Why didn't you take my ten-year-old sister? I don't need her, but I needed my youngest sister so desperately. I loved her so much, but more important than that, she loved me!'" You see, she wasn't receiving the love she needed from her mommy and daddy, and her little sister's love and dependence upon her had compensated. So I said, "Let's allow Jesus to come in and heal it."

I expected Jesus to walk up behind her, but as we looked, He came walking across the yard toward the window. He walked over to where Mary was standing on the inside looking out. Then He simply raised the window, reached in and lifted her through the window. He took this little twelve-year-old in His arms and just loved her and held her for a while. Then He set her down and took her by the hand and they began to walk. It seemed they were just going to talk and talk but after a while the heavens began to open (we didn't try to see this, God was simply allowing us to see what He was doing spiritually to heal her hurt).

There was a pathway — stairway leading up to heaven, and they kept right on walking. When they came to where they were to enter behind the clouds, I knew I could not go with them any further and they stepped out of sight. After some time they reappeared and this is what she told me. When they stepped behind the clouds into heaven, her grandmother and her little four-year-old sister were waiting for her. Mary said, "You know, my little sister wasn't sick any more. She was whole, and she was well! As I left she said, 'We'll all be together again soon'" (including the other sister). Then she and Jesus walked out from behind the clouds, down the pathway to the ground, and back to that same window. Jesus picked her up in His arms, hugged her and loved her, set her back through the window, pulled it down and walked away. The prayer visioning ended just as it had begun with her looking out of the window, but with an entirely different feeling and perspective. Rather than glaring in anger at God for taking her sister, she was praising Him for her sister's complete healing and that one day they would be together again.

As a result of this supernatural healing, Mary went that afternoon to try to see her other sister, but she was too busy. Her sister was afraid to be around her much because of the tension between them. Mary was persistent and continued trying, because she knew her sister was leaving town in a few days. She went back again. Finally catching her at home her sister agreed to see her for a few moments (she was trying to cut down the possibility of a confrontation). This younger sister also had a little daughter who was sickly and whom Mary had never been able to really love because she reminded her of her dead sister. She had never really spontaneously hugged her niece in all of her life, but that afternoon as she came into her house, she put her arms lovingly around her sister and then very emotionally lifted her little niece in her arms and said "I love you." The younger sister called me and said, "I don't know what you and Mary have been doing, but I want to tell you something. Today for the first time my sister hugged me and told me that she loved me! I don't know what you are doing, but oh God, I'm so happy! For the first time in my life I know that my sister really cares!" As the tears flowed on the other end of the phone, she said to me, "Thank you for giving me back my sister."

## **His Healing for You**

Of course I didn't give her back anything, Jesus did. He knows where we hurt, He cares about where we hurt, and He wants to heal us where we hurt. I don't know how you feel about it, but this I know, God loves you. There is no one in the world He loves more than He loves you and no one's hurt which He wants to heal more than He wants to heal yours. He can come into those hurts and heal them right now releasing the anger and resentment that is buried down deep inside setting you free!

God has been showing you where you hurt and there has been some emotion in what I have been sharing, but it has not been designed to be emotional. I don't have any concern about arousing you emotionally, but when I see God's love it moves me. The deepest feelings that are being moved in you are not emotional; they are spiritual. God is reaching out to you in love, to heal you where you hurt, at the point of your deepest need.

I've seen alcoholics and drug addicts set free with hardly any discussion of the addiction. Hardcore homosexuals transformed as Jesus just came in and healed their hurts. We did not major on the symptoms; Jesus just healed the hurts and set them free. I've seen women who have been raped by their father, their brother, their uncle — you name it and it has happened and Jesus has healed them and set them free.

If there is anger, resentment or bitterness inside of you and you have recognized it, it comes from hurts down deep inside which God wants you to recognize, not to make you hurt more, but rather that you might reach out to Him for His healing release.

## A HEALING PRAYER

Father, we lift every need of the person reading these words. So much hurt and rejection needs to be healed and anger and resentment released. And Father, I know that most of it doesn't stem from a planned conspiracy on anybody's part — we simply fail to express our love the way people need us to do. The fact we're rejected doesn't mean they don't care; it just means that so many times it was never adequately communicated.

Father, I ask you to come in right now, and do what I can't do, what no one but you can do. I ask you to let them see you come over, reach down and lift them up, taking them into your arms. I pray that everyone who reads these words will be able to see or sense you putting your arms around them and loving them where they are. Where a particular memory has surfaced, I ask you to come in and remove the hurt and sting. Heal the hurt and meet that need as only you can, allowing all of Calvary's love to flow into their wounds.

Thank you Father for making your love real once again. Amen.

*Chapter 4*

# HOW TO CONQUER YOUR FEARS

A summer rainstorm was in progress as an inner healing service continued — nothing unusual and nothing about which to be concerned. But as a clap of thunder reverberated close by, it was obvious to me that an attractive lady in the congregation had a fear of storms. Her fear was apparent as God instructed me to pray for her. The healing took only a few minutes and as she testified the next night a fear of many years had been supernaturally healed.

## *Fear of People*

Another woman came for counseling who had such a fear of people (and especially men) that she would sit in her apartment alone with the lights out, shades drawn and door bolted (in the daytime) literally shaking with fear at the sound of any passing man's footsteps on the sidewalk outside. She had been molested by both her brothers and her uncle as a child and had hardly been able to function in the years that followed when in the presence of most men. But, praise God, that devastating fear was healed in the first session and what a difference it made in her marriage relationship with her husband. She was soon freed sufficiently to take a job (working mostly with men) and progress to a managerial level.

A salesman came who had a fear in a certain aspect of his work which had limited him professionally for twenty years. God healed him of the fear that day and released him from a heavy dependence upon tranquilizers.

How many similar experiences there have been with those suffering from fear of heights, falling, failure, drowning, animals, loneliness, traveling, dying, confrontation, darkness, and on and on. God wants to heal our fears. The Bible makes clear that this negative kind of fear is not of God (II Timothy 1:7) and is the arch enemy of His agape love and peace being manifested in our lives (I John 4:18; Philippians 4:6,7).

## *Jesus Promises His Peace*

The night before His crucifixion, Jesus spoke directly to this matter of His children being fearful in both John 14:1 and 27 — the latter verse reading "... Let not your heart be troubled, nor let it be fearful" (NASB). He tells us that His peace can prevent our fears and it is not dependent upon our circumstances, because its source is within, not without. It is literally a process of Him giving us His peace — one that goes beyond our understanding and human resources.

There's an excellent little book entitled None of These Diseases by Dr. S. I. MacMillan. If you don't have it, it would be a real blessing to you to find it, read it, and to use it. I want to quote from the preface: "Peace does not come in capsules. This is regrettable because medical science recognizes that emotions such as fear, and sorrow, and envy, resentment and hatred, are responsible for the majority of our sicknesses. The estimates vary from 60% to nearly 100% of all our physical illnesses coming from fear and anger." Such a realization can be disturbing and is considered negative to some people, but I think it is extremely exciting, because God is in the business of healing, not only physically and spiritually, but emotionally as well.

## *Healing for All Areas*

One of the most beautiful and relevant passages in the scriptures at this point is Isaiah 53:5 (KJV) which reads "by His stripes we are healed." In verse 4 it also says, "surely He has borne our griefs and carried our sorrows" on the cross. I believe that this is a direct reference to inner healing, the healing of our emotional hurts and woundings. God is concerned about every area of our being. He loves all of us. The church traditionally has interpreted this passage, to refer to spiritual healing or salvation, and that's what it has historically taught. In recent years a growing number are proclaiming its message of physical healing also, but I believe it includes every dimension of our life: spiritual, physical, and emotional. We have no hurt with which God is not concerned. We have no need which God does not want to meet. As we become aware of this and really learn how to allow God to meet our emotional needs and heal them, we will experience much physical and spiritual healing also.

## *Physical Needs Healed*

This happens all the time in our inner healing counseling. Frequently, God will say in the midst of a session, "I want you to pray for that person's physical needs," when I have no knowledge of what those needs are. So I ask them about their physical needs and pray with them, believing that God wants to heal them physically as well as emotionally. Frequently we see beautiful healing take place — the eyes of the blind opened — everything imaginable! God is a good God!

I remember a woman who was having severe problems in her marriage relationships, it was about to explode in divorce. It was on a Monday and I said, "I want you to come back on Wednesday because we have to gain momentum in these problem areas so God can turn this thing around." She replied, "I can't come back Wednesday." Her reply amazed me in light of the severity of her problem, especially since I offer to see very few people twice in one week. She knew that, and I said "Why not?" Her reply was, "I injured my left knee and ankle severely about two and a half months ago and it's been swollen ever since. I can hardly walk on it and I have an appointment that morning with an orthopedic specialist whom I've been waiting to see for weeks. I just can't come back; I must see him." God spoke to my spirit (otherwise I would not have made this kind of statement), and I said, "Fine. I'll pray for you and God will heal you, and then you can cancel it, and return here on Wednesday." It was very matter of fact. (I don't make that kind of statement except when I feel it rise up in my spirit.) I prayed for her, and she left without saying anything concerning her knee. Many times when God heals, we don't know it at that moment and may not feel anything emotionally or physically. She called rather sheepishly the next morning to say she would be in Wednesday morning. Upon arriving she said, "I don't understand it, but all the swelling went down and the soreness is gone and I don't have any problem with my knee so I cancelled the appointment."

## *What a Miracle!*

A man had come four hundred miles for inner healing, and his problem was so severe a psychiatrist had recently said it would take at least ten years of therapy to have any hope of a real change in his life. He had molested all his daughters and had deep emotional problems and hurts. The oldest daughter, who was in elementary school, had gone to the same psychiatrist and the mother was told it would take two to five years of therapy before she would be able to have anything to do with her father again. But God had other plans and after only one inner healing session the daughter talked of how much she loved her daddy and wanted to see him again! The father and I spent two Saturday afternoons together totaling about nine or ten hours, and God transformed his life. It has been three years since God reconciled his marriage and restored his family with a deep love between he and his wife and daughters.

In the first session, as he and I were talking and praying, God said to me, "Pray for his physical needs." I asked him if he had some, and he told me that throughout childhood and into the teen years he had a severe bed wetting problem. "I've outgrown that," he continued, "but the doctors say that I have a small bladder and I still have a problem in that area" (He was a big, burly construction worker). He said, "The last thing that I do before I leave the jobsite in the afternoon is to go to the bathroom or I will wet my pants on the way home." He was laughing about it (one of those times when you laugh on the outside and cry on the inside), but there is no father who goes home to his wife and children like that and is not deeply hurt by it. And so God said, "Pray for his bladder to be stretched," even though I told Him I didn't know how to pray for a bladder to be stretched. I don't know to this day what happened, except that I was willing to do what God said to do. I told him what God had said for me to pray and my reply to Him, and that He said to do it anyway. So I did. I laid my hands on his lower back and prayed for him for about a minute or two. Then I said, "God has healed you and you're not going to have any more problems with it." In the hour and forty-five minutes we had been together up to that point he had had to use the bathroom twice. The third time should have been coming up, but he didn't have to go. He never had to go again during the three and a half hours of counseling that followed. He drove home nearly 400 miles, called me on the phone and said, "You aren't going to believe this, but I didn't have to go to the bathroom the whole trip!" That was three years ago, and he hasn't had any problem with his bladder since.

It doesn't always happen this simply and easily, but if we will open up to the possibility of what God wants to do, it is beautiful to see him work; furthermore, we learn not to be disappointed or discouraged if we don't see instant results. No one always sees results like that, but the more we are open to God, the more we will see happen, and know that He is desirous of doing more than we've ever dared to dream. God wants us in good health physically, spiritually and emotionally.

## **FEAR IS UNIVERSAL**

He wants us free from every fear that dominates our lives and from the problems they cause us. With that realization in mind, let me share some basic truths in this area with you. The first is that fear is common to all people. Everyone has some fears even though there are people who say they don't. Some are dominated and controlled by them while others do not seem to have any on the surface. Fear is much more subtle and pervasive than any of us have ever fully realized, and is the most powerful weapon in Satan's arsenal.

*Chapter 4: How to Conquer Your Fears*

Each of us has fears of which we are hardly even aware, but this should not be surprising. Our understanding and perception of our emotions is very limited, whether we know it or not. Fear is common to everyone and it began in the Garden of Eden. When Adam and Eve sinned and disobeyed God, and God came walking in the cool of the evening to talk with them, what does the Bible say they did? They were afraid and hid themselves from God. They were afraid to see God, knowing that they had sinned and that fear which began in them has touched the lives of all their descendants. We have all felt the obvious symptoms of fear — the cold, clammy dampness on our hands or other parts of our body, the tightness of the chest, the shakiness in our voice or body, the dryness of mouth, the racing of the heart, the pounding pulse — a lot of different characteristics that we can identify as fear; but many are much more subtle than these and others never see them manifested in us. Each of us have fears we keep buried from the view of others because they are too embarrassing — like fear of the dark, confrontation, rejection, loneliness, insecurity and indecision.

As explained in Chapter 2 in the Inner Healing Reactions Chart, some people are more prone than others and are more likely to have appreciable problems in this area. However, everyone has some problems with fear, because everyone has both fear and anger as part of their basic personality temperament — we are born that way. The most exciting fact, though, is that there is no temperament or personality type which the control of the Holy Spirit cannot modify and strengthen through one of His nine fruit (Galatians 5:22-23). When His peace comes in and His love and joy fill us, fear has to flee! I John 4:18 tells us that His perfect love will cast out all our fear. The Bible says in II Timothy 1:7 that "He has not given us a spirit of fear." (That's what the adversary gives us.) Rather, He has given us "Power and love and a sound mind." We have what we need in Christ to overcome fear as we learn how to walk in the Spirit so that He can control and guide us, healing the hurts in us and setting us free.

Thus, some are more fear-prone by temperament, while others are more fear-prone because of their hurting experiences. I counsel with people all the time who have had terrifying, traumatic experiences. There have been numerous women who have been raped, including those who have been molested by their own fathers, brothers, or other relatives — every kind of traumatic experience you can imagine. Many who as children were physically abused and mistreated in terrible ways. They have traumatic hurts which have created fears and that fear breeds more fear. Fear feeds upon fear and one fear leads to another. If one is fear-prone, he typically might have problems with shyness, insecurity, inferiority, inadequacy, fear of confrontation, and failure as well as many others. One leads to another and they multiply and snowball.

There are thousands and thousands of different kinds of fears. Name any activity and someone somewhere, probably has a fear concerning it.

## *Some Common Fears*

Let me share with you a partial list of fears that are very common (it hardly scratches the surface): fear of heights; of cats and dogs; of animals of all kinds and descriptions; of spiders; of men, women, or children; of being left alone; of storms; of traveling; of leaving the house (numerous individuals have a terrific fear of just leaving their own house or having their children leave the house, to go to school); of insects; of dead bodies; of crowds; of closed in places; of blood; of dying; of marriage (a lot of men have that, don't they?); of pubic speaking; of going crazy; of the dark; of fire; of elevators and escalators; of failure and rejection (even fear of writing a book!). There is fear of poverty, of confrontation; of not being able to sell; of water; or drowning; of horses; of not pleasing others; of being inadequate; of God; of losing one's salvation; of teachers and principals; of going to school (a lot of kids have that); of becoming lost (little children often are afraid that, when their parents leave, they'll get lost or they won't come back); of doctors, dentists, of the boogey man, and on and on and on.

## **FEARS ARE COSTLY**

The various fears are almost endless in number. As I have already stated, fear is the most powerful and pervasive weapon in Satan's arsenal. In some ways that's the most important statement, from a negative standpoint at least, that I'll make in this chapter. There is no weapon that Satan has to use against us that is so powerful and so pervasive as fear. Fear is the Commander-in-Chief of all of Satan's armies. It's a paralyzing poison to our soul (the mind area).

The second basic truth that I would call to your attention is that we pay a high cost for our fears. This is so physically, emotionally, and spiritually. Many doctors estimate that 60% or more of all physical illness is caused by emotional stress, with anger or fear at the root. There is probably no physical illness that cannot be psychosomatically or emotionally induced. You can die from cancer that began because of emotional stress and turmoil. Approximately one-half of the hospital beds in America are occupied by people with emotional problems! It out-weighs all the other illnesses put together. Dr. MacMillan in his book* gives a list of some fifty diseases that are either caused or aggravated by emotional stress. First he lists disorders of the digestive system — ulcers of the mouth, the stomach, the intestines, ulcerative and mucous colitis, loss of appetite, hiccups, constipation, and diarrhea. He continues with disorders of the circulatory system: high blood pressure, arteriosclerosis, coronary thrombosis, gangrene of the legs, rheumatic fever, cerebral strokes of apoplexy. Next, he lists disorders of the genital-urinary system: painful menstruation, lack of menstruation, premenstrual tension and irritability, frigidity, painful coitus, frequent or painful urination, menopausal symptoms and impotence. Additionally, disorders of the nervous system: headaches of several types, alcoholism, epilepsy, psychoneurosis, and insanity, such as schizophrenia and senile dementia. Then he names disorders of glands: internal secretion; hyperthyroidism; diabetes; obesity; allergic disorders like hives and hay fever and asthma; muscle joint disorders like backache, pain and spasm of the muscles; rheumatoid arthritis and osteoarthritis; infectious mononucleosis; and even polio. He names eye diseases like glaucoma, and skin diseases such as hives, atypical dermatitis; neurodermatitis, Reanaulds' disease, scleroderma, Lupus, and psoriasis, as well as many, many others.

Emotional factors such as fear will many times hinder the healing that God has for us and yet are often never even considered as a casual factor. On the other hand, many times when a medical doctor cannot find the problem physically, he simply says, "It's all in your head," which is very unfortunate. There may be a lot of truth in such a statement because the real battle is in our minds, but to say it's all in the mind is too frequently a cop-out for the doctor and condemnation for the patient. Traditionally, emotional illnesses have been much more difficult to heal than physical ones and they are even more widespread.

## *Fear Affects Circulation*

Fear and anxiety can place tremendous stress on the heart. There are many things that contribute to heart attacks and heart-related problems — cholesterol, overweight, lack of exercise, smoking, drinking, etc. — but doctors are coming back to the fact that perhaps the greatest single cause of heart-related problems and diseases is emotional stress, growing out of anger and fear. Stress has been shown to increase the clotting of the blood which contributes to heart attacks. A medical study* was made some time ago of one hundred fifty people that I want to share with you. They were divided into three groups of fifty each to study the clotting of their blood. In what appeared to be fifty normally happy people it took eight to twelve minutes clotting time. With fifty apprehensive ones, it took only four to five minutes for the blood to clot. When fifty highly nervous people were tested, their blood began to clot in only three minutes. Now what does that say? The more nervous and fearful you become, literally, the more one's blood thickens and any existing circulatory problem is greatly aggravated by the thickened blood — the heart has to work overtime. Heart attacks and heart-related illnesses and diseases can be greatly accelerated and compounded by fear. That's why people sometimes die in an extreme moment of fright — they literally drop dead of complications caused by the fear.

## *Fear Destroys Faith*

Problems growing out of fear are endless. We've talked about some of the physical effects, but the emotional effect is even worse. Fear steals the peace that Jesus wants to give us and there is no quiet inside. The peace, a deep pervasive peace that revitalizes and restores the entire body metabolism. Instead of this quiet, there's confusion and indecision in people controlled by their circumstances. Fear produces doubt and unbelief and when we're afraid, we find it very difficult to trust. When we can't trust, we begin to doubt causing unbelief to grow and short-circuit everything which God wants to do in our lives. The Bible says, "Whatsoever is not of faith is sin" (Romans 14:23). Faith is the channel through which God works, and we can't trust God when we're afraid — our fears overwhelm us, they control and dominate us. They produce not only doubt and unbelief, but double-mindedness, worry and anxiety as well.

Several years ago I was talking to a couple who were professing Christians, but filled with fear. She carried a gun in her purse and he carried a gun in his belt, under his coat, all the time — they were so fearful. We talked about the worry and anxiety in their life. After nearly two and a half hours of sharing with them, trying to get through, the woman looked at me as tears welled up in her eyes and began to flow down her cheeks saying, "Well, if worry is sin, I must be the world's greatest sinner!" She was consumed with worry and anxiety that grew out of fear.

Fear breeds tension and nervousness which consume all the good things in one's life, fostering disappointment, discouragement, despondency, despair, defeat, and depression. A woman came in to my office with eyes recessed, with a zombie-like look, walking very slowly and methodically — in deep depression. This had been going on for months and she did not know what to do. She was a fine Christian woman who loved the Lord. A series of rejections over the last few months had triggered that sense of rejection which was already present and drove her into depression. We talked and prayed together for nearly two hours and she left rejoicing because God had begun to break the depression and had started turning things around. But there was much more inner healing to do to prevent the depression from recurring. It occurs as the culmination of a series of negative experiences and can only be completely broken and healed by eliminating the root of the problem which is a sense and fear of rejection producing growing self-pity. The central symptom is self-centeredness or preoccupation with our own problems.

## *Don't Focus on the Shadows*

Psalm 23 says 'Though I walk through the valley of the shadow of death I will fear no evil" and the exciting thing is that a valley is open-ended. A valley is not a box-end canyon, and God says "When I walk with you, it's always open-ended — just keep your eyes on me." Our problems come not from having "valley" experiences, but in the fact that as we walk through those valleys we tend to focus our attention on the "shadows" rather than the sunlight. Supposedly, a study was done a few years ago where a lot of information was fed into a computer and the results stated that 92% of the things we worry about never occur. There is a lot of truth in that, and most of us are aware of it. Worry, basically, is toward the future. We're fearful of what may or may not happen in the future. God says, "Live one day at a time." (James 4:13-15) Jesus said, "Take no thought for tomorrow." (Matthew 6:25) The literal thrust of his statement is "Don't take that fearful thought; don't receive that thought of worry and anxiety, don't let it come against you and take root in your mind and begin to grow and flourish.

Fear is the soil out of which grows all kinds of trouble and problems. Let me list some of them for you briefly: shyness, insecurity, sadness, loneliness, hopelessness, helplessness, inferiority, inadequacy, negativism and doubt, indecision and superstition. Ironically, though we live in a day of great scientific knowledge, sophistication and education, we are becoming more and more pagan and superstitious. How many people measure their lives by the stars? Our churches are filled with people who follow the horoscopes and attend séances. Periodically there are programs on television where the host interviews a psychic. If they have any validity, it is because that power source comes from the adversary, the devil.

Fear also produces problems in the area of laziness, daydreaming, fantasy, escapism, sleeplessness, fatigue, frustration, moodiness, embarrassment, self-pity, perfectionism, hysteria, clumsiness, suicidal tendencies, and masochism, as well as frigidity, impotence, jealousy, overeating, guilt and various addictions of all kinds. Fear can cause almost any kind of problem imaginable. But the beautiful thing is, God wants to liberate us from our fears. Fear destroys everything God wants to do in our lives spiritually. We need to realize that and not accept fear, but learn how to reject it and overcome it.

# CAUSES OF FEAR

Let's review now what I have been saying. We have already discussed that fear is common to everybody and have also talked about the high cost of fear. Now I want us to focus in on the cause of fear. What causes a person to be afraid? Normal fear, on what I call a "response level," is part of our inheritance from God and is a gift from Him. It's built into us as part of our human nature, as not all fear is bad, nor wrong. It's emotionally healthy to sometimes be afraid, or cautious. Maybe "cautiousness" would be a better word than fear to define normal fear, since there are times when we need to be afraid. For instance, if we see a rattlesnake, there should be a sense of cautious fear, though not of panic which can be very dangerous and detrimental to our body metabolism.

An area which contributes greatly to our reacting in fear is negative thinking patterns. So much of our defeat occurs at this point, because the real battle is in the mind, or soul area. The new birth gives us a new spirit, and it must be nurtured on the word of God, fed in spiritual communion with the Father so that it will grow stronger and take authority over the soul area (the mind), bringing it into subjection. Then the soul area, as it is brought under subjection of the Spirit, will in turn bring the body under its control. If we try to change the soul or mind area without feeding and growing the spirit, we will be very limited in our success. The battle takes place in this mind area for it's where Satan attacks and comes against us. He tempts us to the point of our thoughts, and we have to learn, as Paul says in II Corinthians 10:5, to "take every thought captive to the obedience of Christ." This is a process and part of it is to reject the negative thinking patterns which we have developed. (See the author's "5 R's to Victory in Your Thought-Life" in the appendix.)

## *Positive Faith, Not Positive Thinking*

I am not referring to the power of positive thinking. There is power in positive thinking but positive thinking is man's solution to man's problems and God has a better idea. He always does have, and God's solution is to give us a positive spirit of expectancy through the daily control of the Holy Spirit. We don't have to try to be positive to the degree that the Holy Spirit controls us for He produces positive expectancy — it is impossible not to be positive! If I'm down or despondent, I know that my feelings are in control and the Holy Spirit is not, and that I need to put Him back in control. As I do, I no longer see problems, only challenges, and the challenge is to turn that problem over to Jesus, so that His Holy Spirit may work within me in my behalf. Nothing dismays Him, discourages or defeats Him. We are only defeated when we look at our problems and needs in the light of our resources rather than in the light of His resources — the ones God has promised and has already made available to us. We must learn how to feed our faith that it might grow strong and bold. It grows in two ways. The Bible says, "faith comes by hearing and hearing by the word of God." (Romans 10:17) The Bible also says that faithfulness is a fruit of the spirit. (Galatians 5:22) So walking in the Spirit produces the fruit of faithfulness in our lives, and we find ourselves growing in our faith and in our ability to trust Him. Jesus also said in Mark 11:22 that we have this kind of faith in us — His kind of faith. He's already given us this faith, and it's extremely important that we begin to realize what we already possess in Christ and begin to exercise and use it. I don't really think we need more faith nearly as much as we just need to learn how to exercise what faith we already possess in Christ. We have enough faith. He said faith as a grain of mustard seed can literally move mountains. (Matthew 17:20) Whatever the mountain in our life, God can move it, working through our faith. So we need to feed our faith in the word and in communion with the Father so that we can release it when we need it. F. F. Bosworth said, "Most Christians feed their bodies three hot meals a day, and their spirit one cold snack a week and then wonder why they are so weak in faith."

## *Rejection Brings Fear*

Another thing that will hurt us and create fear is fearful experiences in our lives. They just amplify our basic tendencies. If we're already fear-prone and we have fearful, hurting experiences, they are going to make us more afraid, unless we learn how to let God heal them, and take them away. Many of our fears are rooted in experiences of rejection. The rejection can be real or imagined and, to some degree, it is always both. I believe that rejection is the root of all our emotional hurts that involve people. There are two kinds of fears — those which are directly related to people, and those which do not seem to be. I believe that the former are always rooted in experiences that have been perceived as rejection. Repeated rejection creates a sense of rejection in an individual. This grows into a fear of rejection, which is the root of all people-related fears. That fear of rejection in turn progresses into self-criticism and self-rejection, producing self-condemnation and ultimately a low self-image in those areas where we feel rejected.

People say to me all the time, 'I don't have a low self-image." Personally, I don't think there is anyone who doesn't have this problem to some degree. We tend to speak in terms of black and white, and either/or, where the self-image is concerned, but it is always a matter of degree. So we have a low self-image in those areas where we have experienced significant rejection and have developed a fear of it.

Our self-image may be good, even healthy and strong in other areas. There are men who function well in their jobs and have a strong self-image in that area, but they may have a very poor self-image as a father or husband. I know of relatively few men who have a strong self-image at the point of their spiritual leadership in their family. We need to learn to think in terms of degree. We must also come to understand where our self-image is weak and to let God show us how he can heal it so that we might be set free to come into emotional balance and perspective. In these areas where our self-image is weak from rejection and sense of failure, we tend to over-react and to experience our strongest fears.

## GOD HAS A CURE

The exciting thing is that God has a cure for all our fears. It is to be found in Jesus Christ and in God's work. The answer does not lie in positive thinking, traditional psychiatric and psychological counseling, sheer will power, or some ambiguous idea of God. The only lasting answer that brings deep, permanent healing is to be found through the mighty power of God in Jesus Christ.

For instance, in working with drug addicts, we have never had anyone who was not set free of their addictions within a relatively few counseling sessions — set free without extensive concentration on the drug problem. (It is always a surface problem and never a root cause.) We simply heal the load-bearing hurts that God shows us, and the need for the drugs begins to subside. We are so prone to deal with symptoms and surface problems. When we concentrate on an alcoholic's drinking problem, per se, we are "majoring on a minor" in the emotional area. We may get, someone dried out for a while, but he probably will not be healed, because the same hurts which originated the problem will still largely exist. When we let God's Spirit guide us to where the hurts are, and He heals them, then the person is set free from the need of the emotional crutch. The same is so with homosexuality, or any other problem area. God has reiterated over and over again to me that I must not become preoccupied with symptoms and surface problems. He must be allowed to show us where the root problems are, if deep inner healing is to take place. As a result, the person is set free from his fear, anger, resentment, addiction, or whatever the need.

### *Jesus is the Answer*

The answer is found in Jesus Christ and the word of God as it is energized by the Holy Spirit. It's not found in religion at all, nor in some kind of vague, universal concept by God. Our deep needs can only be met by the God of Jesus Christ and

His word to men, the Bible. I John 4:18, which I quoted earlier, says, "His perfect love casts out all fear." I Peter 5:7 says, "Casting all your cares and anxieties upon Him, because He cares for you." He cares for you. He'll take those cares and lift the weight of them off of you. It does not mean he takes them and starts worrying for you, but that He takes them away from you because He doesn't worry about anything. Psalm 34:4 says, "I sought the Lord and He answered me and delivered me from all my fears." Isaiah 26:3 says, "Thou wilt keep him in perfect peace whose mind is stayed on thee."

## *Fear is Sin*

Fear is not of God — it is not of God. It is sin. It is wrong. It is self-destructive and self-defeating. It's devastating and you've only got to learn to identify fear and to identify its source as from the adversary. You must not receive it — do not take that thought, do not receive that fear. "He has not given us a spirit of fear, but of power" (the power we have in Jesus Christ), "and love" (His love that's unconditional with no strings attached), "and of a sound mind" (and you can't have a sound mind when it is filled with fear). (II Timothy 1:7). Fear quenches the Holy Spirit. I Thessalonians 5:19 says, "Quench not the Holy Spirit," and yet we quench the Spirit of God by our fears. Fear forms doubt, which in turn prevents faith, and "whatsoever is not of faith is sin." (Romans 14:23) Fear is sin and we need to understand that, to recognize it and call it what it is — S-I-N.

## *Breaking of Relationships*

Let me tell you what I believe is the essence of sin from the emotional aspect. Sin is anything that breaks relationships. Listen, and let this soak in, because it is not what is taught about sin most of the time. We talk about sin as disobedience or rebellion, and it is, but those are characteristics of sin. They are not the essence of sin emotionally. Sin is the breaking of relationships. God loves people and God is concerned about anything that hurts people. Sin is the breaking of relationships between a person and himself, other and God. It is the breaking of relationships which hurts people, hurts us and hurts the heart of God. Sin breaks the heart of God because it hurts people and God is basically concerned about things as they relate to people. To take what belongs to someone else hurts God because it hurts that person and anything which mars and scars our relationship with God, ourselves and others is sin.

Sin is "missing the mark," as the New Testament teaches. In fact, it's missing everything that's really worthwhile in life. It is missing God's whole perspective on life and that's bad with a capital "B." It is a wrong reaction that is wrong for everybody concerned. It is self-defeating and destructive to everyone involved — no wonder sin is so wrong!

## *Confession—The Key*

The Bible is very clear about what we must do with our sins and wrong reactions. We must confess them. I John 1:9 says, "If we confess our sins, He is faithful and righteous to forgive us our sins and to cleanse us from all unrighteousness." The next verse continues, "If we say that we have not sinned we make Him a liar, and His word is not in us." The apostle John was not writing to lost people and that's how Christians tend to interpret those verses. He was talking to born-again believers, and emphatically stating that continual confession must become a way of life. Every time we sin we have to confess it. We have to release it and if we don't, it just builds up inside of us. It becomes like a brick that drops in between us and God. They begin to pile up and build a wall between us and God, and they cut us off from Him. Not, cut us off in the sense of losing our salvation, but in breaking our fellowship. It short-circuits our communication and breaks our contact with God so that we cannot hear Him as clearly. Thus, we cannot be as sensitive, or as responsive to Him. Sin breaks that relationship between us and God in the sense of our intimacy, communion and communication.

## *Agree with God*

Remember what I told Billy in Chapter 2 what confession means? It means to agree with God, to agree with God that what He is saying to you is right. God is talking to us all the time because He loves us! Much of the problem is that we haven't really learned how to listen! How could He love us and care about us and not talk to us? The meaning of the word "confession," literally, is prefaced on that fact. How can we agree with God about something if God isn't saying anything to us? So we must learn how to agree with God — that what He is saying to us is right.

More and more I'm learning that when I hear God say something to immediately respond "God, you're right. I may not understand why you're right, or how you are right, but I know you're right!" I save myself a lot of time and wasted effort when I start with that assumption, that fact — that God is right. So begin agreeing with God. You don't need a "feeling" because confession does not necessarily involve any emotional feeling. That's another area where we miss it; we think that we have to feel like confessing. People say "I'll accept Christ, I'll confess Jesus Christ as Savior, when I have a certain kind of feeling, or when I have the kind of experience that

Paul had on the road to Damascus." Well, we may wait forever for that feeling, because God doesn't tend to give feelings in advance. God gives the right feeling when we do the right thing, and if we don't do the right thing, we aren't going to get the right feeling! Not from God! The devil will play with our emotional feelings and sometimes he will give us what we think is the right feeling to stop us short of what God wants us to do. The devil deals in emotional feelings, and God deals with spiritual feelings. The only feelings that we can count on are the feelings that come from our spirit and we must learn how to discern them.

## *Repentance Is Not A Feeling*

This kind of confession always involves repentance, but repentance is not an emotion either; it's not a feeling; it's an act of our will by faith and a change of mind. So when we repent, we stop arguing with God, we stop copping out, and we say, "God, you're right, I'm wrong." That's confession and repentance all rolled into one (re-read the story of Billy in Chapter 2). We cannot biblically confess without biblically repenting. If we confess properly, we line up with God and agree with Him and in that process we have also repented. God says recognize fear as sin and confess, "God, you're right, I am afraid; this is the way I feel, it's wrong, I'm sorry for it and I release it to you."

This is stepping out by faith. And faith involves risk-taking. So we'll never overcome our fears without taking some risks. People who are fearful do not want to take risks, but even the turtle doesn't get anywhere without sticking out his neck. We can't walk on water if we don't get out of the boat. It is risky to walk with Jesus, but deeply rewarding. The fear has to be removed, the thought of fear rejected, and the spirit of fear rebuked. When fear is causing us real problems, we can know there's a spirit of fear involved. An evil spirit is just like a germ where the emotions are concerned. When we have a physical wound, a germ will come in and take up residence in it and infecting and worsening it if we don't sterilize and cover it so it can heal. The germ did not cause the wound, nor originate it; it simply took advantage of it, and worsened and infected it — an evil spirit is the same way. If we have an emotional wound, where we have been hurt by someone and have anger, fear, resentment, bitterness, etc., a corresponding spirit will come in much like a germ and take up residence in it. It does not cause the emotional wound but simply aggravates and amplifies it. The devil does not make us do anything. We do it! We do it by forfeiting our authority over him and in ignorance or otherwise, cooperating with him. If we have anger stewing inside of us, we can know that there is a spirit of anger involved. When we have fear, the same way. So we need to reject the thought of fear, rebuke the spirit of fear, and replace them with positive thoughts and confessions from the word of God.

Utilize passages like Philippians 4:8 and 9, which go to the heart of this matter. "Finally, brethren, whatsoever is true, whatever is honorable, whatever is right, whatever is pure, whatever is lovely, whatever is of good repute, if there by any excellence, and anything worthy of praise, let your mind dwell on these things — practice these things and the God of peace shall be with you." (NASB) This is thinking positively according to the Spirit of God and in the Word of God, not psyching ourselves up with man's ideas, but simply feeding on the Word and its positive teachings. When we do, we'll find fear being dispelled and cast out by His perfect love.

## Fears Flee

Sometimes the fear experience has to be healed for us to be set free. I could stand here and spend hours telling you about experiences of people being healed of fears. The first experience of inner healing that I knowingly had, dealt with my previously terrible fear of falling. (It was discussed in some detail in Chapter 2) It controlled me and I could not control it. Through a prayer vision He set me free of a twenty five year old trauma in less than two minutes!

A young man had been homosexually raped as a child and God healed him of that tragic experience in the first session! Jesus set him free!

Another woman had a fear of death from seeing and touching her grandfather's body in the casket as a small girl. God brought back that memory, then Jesus walked up to the casket with her and He touched her granddad. Then He let her touch him, and he explained it to her and healed that hurting memory in moments.

A young lady remembered how she came home from elementary school one afternoon to find police cars and an ambulance. As she came up the porch steps, they were bringing her mother out on a stretcher. She had one glance at her mother's anguished face. It said to this little girl, "I'll never see you again." They took the mother to the hospital, but would not allow the child to see or be by her mother's side, because she wasn't old enough to go into the room. The mother died a few hours later. She remembered the agony of that funeral, never understanding what had happened to her mommy. Over and over she would see them lowering the casket into the cold, dark earth. Ever since then she had been haunted by the face of her mother, and that look. Oh, God, how she wished she could have been with her mommy! Jesus came in to that experience supernaturally in prayer visioning.

He took her into the hospital room and over to the mother's bedside, and let them love each other. Then He took her out to the grave site, opened up the casket, and her mother was not in it. Jesus said, "She's already in heaven with me, and you will be too, one day." Now I don't understand how that healed her, but it did! Jesus did it, and she's never had any hurt nor fear in that area since.

## *Steel in Her Stomach*

While teaching in another city a woman shared that she had a fear of riding in an automobile. She would become very nervous, especially if there was a close call, like the screeching of brakes. God brought back a couple of experiences of being in automobile accidents and healed them, and I thought we were through at first. However, there was a "check" in my spirit and I said, "No, there's another memory that God's trying to bring back that goes much deeper into your past." She began to cry out and sob, as she said, "Yes, my daddy was killed in an automobile accident when I was six months old!" Jesus came in to that and healed her and set her free! When we got through she looked at me as she wiped the tears away and smiled the most radiant smile. She said, "You have no idea what this has done for me. All of my life I've felt like I had a piece of cold steel right in the pit of my stomach and I never understood what it was. Now it's gone because Jesus healed me of the hurt of my daddy's death." God is so good!

Another woman who had a deep fear of men had just been divorced from her husband. She could hardly have anything to do with men because she had been hurt by men so much, beginning with her father. God healed the related memories and set her free that day. God frees us from every kind of fear — fear of dark, fear of men, fear of being in front of a class (so many children have been hurt in school as teachers have inadvertently embarrassed them in front of the class). God removed my fear when He took me back to the third and fifth grades in prayer with Ed and Betty Tapscott and showed me two experiences which He healed. The teacher didn't mean to hurt me. She didn't understand how much it was affecting me when she laughed at the way I said a word, and then the whole class began to laugh because of the teacher. That fear had been there for years and was almost impossible to overcome at times. But, praise God, no more!

## *An Attitude of Gratitude*

A final aspect which is so important to our healing relates to our having an attitude of gratitude. I Thessalonians 5:18 says, "Rejoice in all things, for this is the will of God in Christ Jesus concerning you." What happens to us is not necessarily the will of God, but rejoicing in everything is the will of God. Romans 8:28 says "All things work together for good to them that love the Lord." As we rejoice in all things, we can begin to look for the good which is pregnant within every experience. God is in the business of turning bad into good, bringing triumph out of tragedy, and turning defeat into victory.

Remember what Philippians 4:4, 6, 7 said? "Rejoice in the Lord always, and again I say, Rejoice. Be anxious for nothing, but in everything by prayer and supplication with thanksgiving let your request be made known unto God and the peace of God which surpasses all comprehension shall guard your hearts and your minds in Christ Jesus." Cultivate an attitude of gratitude in all things! It will pay rich dividends in your life.

## A HEALING PRAYER

Father, we thank you for your healing touch. We thank you that you are not only our Creator, Redeemer and Lord, but also our Great Physician. We thank you, Father, that there is no need in our life which you do not desire to meet and no hurt which you do not want to heal.

I thank you that you know and love everyone who reads these words. You know their every need. And so I ask you to minister to them by your Holy Spirit. We claim the promise of your word — "not by might, nor by (human) power, but by your Spirit." We praise you!

Where there is fear of darkness, or water, or death — we ask you to come in, Lord Jesus putting your arms around and loving the reader and heal their fear. For those with fear of men we ask you, the Man of Galilee, to love them healing the fear, and breaking that bondage. Let those who fear the loss of their salvation know your love and experience it in Jesus beyond anything they've known up to this point. For that fear of rejection which is in the hearts and minds of so many, Father, we ask you to help them to know how totally and completely you love and accept them — with no strings attached. Help them understand that there's nothing they can ever do to cause you to stop loving them. Bathe and immerse them in your love that they might be set free — liberated in Christ.

Father, for those whose fear has led to a spirit of sadness, melancholy and heaviness in their life, we ask that you might massage them with the oil of gladness and lift that spirit of heaviness. Give them a garland of gladness, praise, and thanksgiving. No matter where those fears came in — through their temperament, in the fetus, in the early years of their life, elementary school, or junior high, high school or college, in their marriage relationship, in their business associations or wherever — we ask you to touch and to heal and to set free.

We rebuke and bind ever hindering, harassing and resisting spirit, every spirit of fear that would dominate and destroy. We command every spirit of shyness, and insecurity, inferiority, and inadequacy to leave in Jesus' name! The sense of hopelessness and helplessness, that deep permeating sense of desolation, that aching, deep, deep inside — we take authority over each of these in Jesus' name and command them to leave. And we thank you Father for that release.

Where there is fear of confrontation, failure, people or financial distress, we ask you to lovingly minister. We release your healing balm to meet every need. We thank you that you are supplying all these needs, according to your riches in glory by Christ Jesus (Philippians 4:19). We thank you and praise you, Father.

You have said in your word that your "perfect love casts out all fear." (I John 4:18)

Thank you that it's being done! You've also said that you "have not given us the spirit of fear, but of power and love and a sound mind" (II Timothy 1:7), and we thank you, Father, that your Holy Spirit is allowing your love and power and joy and peace to flow in to meet all of these needs, releasing them supernaturally into our lives, giving us that sound mind and self-control which comes only through your Holy Spirit. We thank you and praise you in Jesus' name. Amen.

*Chapter 5* 

# HOW TO FORGIVE AND THEN FORGET

Forgiveness is a tremendously important topic in Jesus' teaching. An interesting passage on this subject is the conversation between Jesus and Peter in Matthew 18:21, "Then Peter came and said to Jesus, 'Lord, how often shall my brother sin against me and I forgive him, up to seven times?' Jesus said to him, 'I do not say to you up to seven times but up to seventy times seven.'" Then He goes on to tell a parable about forgiveness. What was Peter doing? He was wanting to know when he had done enough, when he had forgiven others enough to meet Jesus' standards. Have you ever had that question? Ever had anyone bug you so badly that you wanted to know what your obligations before God were? When would it be enough so that even God would be satisfied?

Peter knew the Jewish law taught we should forgive a person three times. So he said, "Lord, is seven times enough?" He probably expected to really impress Jesus. "Certainly this would be going the second mile." Jesus has the most terrific way of deflating us when we are filled with pride. He said, "not seven, but seventy times seven.'2 What He was saying was we need only to forgive others as long as we want God to forgive us. Forgiveness is not so much for the benefit of the other person, as it is to help us! He is teaching how tremendously important and therapeutic forgiveness is for you and me. It isn't that God needs us to do it or that we are primarily to do it for the sake of others. We pre-eminently need to do it for ourselves (Mark 11:25-26).

## WE NEED TO FORGIVE

That's the first of three key concepts which I want to impress upon you in this chapter. We need to forgive. There are no exceptions to this because we have all been hurt and/or offended by others at times. We cannot live in this world without it — It's inevitable. Hurts, disappointments and rejection are an inescapable fact of life. The really insignificant ones can sometimes be forgotten, but many have been buried in our subconscious mind. As I've already said, I believe that we have total recall in our subconscious mind of anything significant which has ever happened to us. In that sense each of us has photographic memory. Those hurts affect us and have left their mark on our lives in various ways. In fact, they infect our lives. They have caused us to have emotional scar tissue which needs to be cut away. If it's not, it can be damaging to us spiritually and physically, as well as emotionally.

Peggy is an example. She was married, a mother and hurting. One of the memories which the Spirit brought back to the surface had emotional scar tissue dating to when she was six years old. Her mother had divorced her father and Peggy was very insecure — mommy was her only security blanket.

Hurrying home at lunch from first grade she burst into the house only to be greeted by silence. The house was empty and mommy was gone. On the kitchen table was a can of soup which she could not open and a note which she could not read (Mother had gone shopping with a friend). Resentment followed rejection, resentment towards this unknown woman who had taken mommy away and resentment towards mommy — both for being gone when she needed her and for divorcing daddy and sending him away.

Buried for many years and covered with emotional scar tissue it was still festering, hurting and unhealed. That day she not only confessed these feelings, but the little girl in her finally forgave mommy and the woman, was set free.

## *Self-Defeating and Self-Punishment*

God's means of removal involves forgiving. Not to forgive is self-defeating and self-destructive. It is counterproductive and will short-circuit His ability to give us the abundant life we desire. In fact, as I've stated before, it is wrong. Wrong because it's bad. Bad, because it's bad for us. What it so frequently boils down to is self-punishment.

Who does it hurt most? Not forgiving others hurts us. We are cutting ourselves from God and His forgiveness of us. It establishes a wall of unforgiveness between us and Him that not even God Himself can circumvent. He wants to, but He can't. Our unforgiving spirit acts like a dam that blocks the flow of His forgiveness to us. The river of His love and forgiveness is turned into a dead sea by our spirit of unforgiveness.

It is also self-punishment because it allows the ones who have already hurt us to go on hurting us. The anger and resentment we feel towards them continues to stress us and allows the memory of their actions to continue to pull our emotional strings — it follows us wherever we go. It is critically important that we come to realize how imperative it is for us to forgive others, not so much for their sake as for our own. To not do so is to program ourselves for failure, emotionally, physically, and spiritually.

*Chapter 5: How to Forgive and Then Forget*

# FORGIVEN SO WE CAN FORGIVE

The second key point that I would stress with you in this chapter is that we must be forgiven to be able to forgive. Only the forgiven can forgive. This is so because we simply cannot pass on what we do not have. That's a fact of life in any area. Let's use the financial aspect as an illustration. Suppose I had a will drawn up by an attorney and in that will I stated that I was leaving my wife and children a million dollars. That would be fine, except for one small matter — I do not have a million dollars, therefore I cannot leave it to them in my will, because I cannot pass on to them that which I do not possess.

As another example, let's say that I was scheduled to teach a class on Einstein's Theory of Relativity. Everyone could show up including me, but it would be to no avail. I do not know or understand his theory and, thus, could not possibly teach it to a class. Why? Because we cannot pass along that which we do not possess. It's an immutable law of life.

To be able to forgive others (especially in the areas of load-bearing hurts), we must first receive forgiveness from God. All forgiveness originates with Him, as does everything spiritual, love, mercy, salvation. It is important that we understand that forgiveness is basically spiritual and not emotional. The essence of it is not a feeling, but a willful act of faith which is God-like. We can only forgive after we have received His forgiveness in that particular area of deep hurt. It is only possible for us to forgive at all, because he first forgave us. By forgiving someone else we are being Christ-like and literally "conforming to the image of Christ." We are also in a very practical sense doing that which is best for us. Forgiveness, like the baton in a relay race, must be passed on. In passing along His forgiveness, we are recognizing its similarity to the manna provided the Israelites in the wilderness. It cannot be stored or hoarded, only received, used and shared. Every blessing from God comes to us on its way to someone else.

Now the crucial question becomes, "How do we receive this forgiveness from God so that we may be able to pass it on to others and thereby release ourselves in that area of binding hurt?" I John 1:9 makes this very clear. "If we confess ... He is faithful and just to forgive... and to cleanse us. . ." What we must do to receive His forgiveness is to confess our sin or wrong reaction. When we do, it's automatic. Our confession pulls down the damming wall and allows His forgiveness to flow into our hurting memory as a cleansing, healing balm.

## Confession is the Key

It is so imperative that we come to see that the key to forgiveness is confession. To try to forgive without having confessed means we are attempting to pass on something which we do not possess. This is pre-eminently so in the area of load-bearing hurts. When someone else has hurt us and we finally come around to dealing with it spiritually, we tend to try to forgive without confessing. After all, we know that they were primarily at fault! What is there for us to confess? — our wrong reactions to what they did to us. Remember the discussion about this in Chapter 2 and the illustration of it through "The Story of Billy." Go back and re-read it carefully if you do not fully understand the concept and necessity of confessing your wrong reactions.

## Us—Not Them

To be able to "forgive and forget," we must quit concentrating on what the other person did to us and focus on what our negative feelings were concerning their actions. We are only responsible for our attitudes and actions, not theirs. It is so important that we understand this. This is all that God holds us accountable for, and the essence of what must be dealt with to release us. We can never be healed of our hurts until we begin to realize this and deal with it on this basis. It is the confession of our sin and wrong reactions which brings forgiveness to us, and allows us to pass that forgiveness on to those who have hurt us.

## Be Specific, But Don't Dig

This type of confession needs to be specific, not general. We need to deal with specific experiences and specific hurting memories (there is no more power in general confession than there is in general prayer). Ask and expect God to bring back to your conscious mind those festering, hurting memories that are down in your subconscious mind. Don't dig and dredge for them, or go into deep introspection. Approach this area of your need as in all others ... in a posture of faith. God wants you well and wants to do inner healing within you. Since this requires the healing of memories, God will bring back those memories which need to be healed as you are able to handle them and ready to release them. So be patient, and walk with him in expectancy. Set aside time daily for communion with the Father, and as you wait before Him He will periodically speak to you in this area. Also, be ready for memories to come out of the blue. Seize hold of them, examine them, and deal with them in the three steps to inner healings. Confession of our wrong reactions is simply the first step in this healing process.

## *Sterilize, Then Stitch*

As we confess, his forgiveness is released like a healing antiseptic to come in and cleanse our emotional wound (I John 1:9). When we try to forgive without confessing, it is like stitching up an infected wound. It will not hold, and we will be unable to "forget." Our confession brings his forgiveness, which cleanses and sterilizes our wound. It is like the doctor's use of peroxide and iodine in our physical wounds. Only after the infection has been removed are we ready to be able to effectively forgive. Just as sterilization must precede stitching physically, so must confession precede forgiveness emotionally. This is pre-eminently so with the healing of our load-bearing hurts. Come to think of confession and forgiveness as Siamese's twins — inseparable. They are two sides of the same coin. When we have confessed, then and only then are we ready to close off the wound to further problems of infection through the process of unilateral forgiveness. During the process of inner healing forget about trying to forgive people simply because it's noble, let alone because they deserve it. Jesus did not forgive because people deserved it. They frequently don't! He forgave because it was in His own best interests to do so, and because it is God-like. Never in the pages of the New Testament did anyone apologize to Jesus and ask His forgiveness, but He always gave it. He forgave unilaterally out of His own being because it was right for both Him and them. He gave it because it was right for Him to do so, and to prevent an attitude of unforgiveness from developing within Him and thus short-circuiting all of the Father's plans. And that's exactly what an unforgiving spirit does in you and me — it short-circuits God's attempt to give us an abundant life. To not forgive allows the one who has hurt us to go on indirectly controlling our lives. It lets them "pull our strings." Can you imagine what would have happened if Jesus had not forgiven Herod or Judas?

It is important, too, that we come to realize how deep and rich His forgiveness is when we confess. The Bible says that he removes our sins as far as the East is from the West (Psalm 103:12). It is impossible to really understand how far that is, but let me use an illustration to assist us.

## *Gone, Gone, Gone*

Our solar system with its sun and planets is only one of a countless number in the universe, and ours is one of the smaller solar systems at that. Our system along with many others together compose what is known as the Milky Way Galaxy, and it, in turn, is one of the smaller of countless galaxies in this universe. Yet, in spite of this, the size of our galaxy is beyond our human comprehension.

For instance, if we could board a rocket ship traveling at the speed of light (approximately 186,000 miles per second) it would take us 200 million years just to make one trip around this Milky Way! Unbelievable and yet that distance would not begin to approach how far it is from the East to the West in our universe. And the Bible says that that's how far He takes our sins and wrong reactions away! Oh, Glory!

A recent prayer visioning experience comes to mind. A lovely, but hurting lady was having a difficult time forgetting her own sin. She was afraid that even after she confessed it that it would come back to haunt her. As we went to God in prayer for a deep healing He allowed us to see what Jesus was doing to give her sufficient assurance.

In the spirit we saw her and Jesus on a rocket ship chasing after her confessed sins. They were traveling at 186,000 miles per second (our moon rockets travel at about 15,000-20,000 miles per hour by comparison!), but could not catch them. Her sins were moving away at an even faster rate, being taken as far as the East is from the West. They just kept falling further behind as the sins soared completely out of sight! What a healing release took place inside of her that day. When we confess, and He forgives, our sins are literally no more. God's mercy is beyond comprehension, and all forgiveness is rooted in His infinite, undeserved mercy towards us.

## *A Second Kind*

Earlier in this chapter we discussed one of the two kinds of load-bearing hurts which we have inside of us, the type that develops basically from someone else hurting us. They are primarily at fault. When we finally come around to dealing with it on a spiritual level, as I said, we tend to try to forgive them, but usually do not think in terms of confessing anything on our part. The other kind of load-bearing hurt, which we've not discussed here, stems from our hurting someone else by our actions. When we finally begin to deal with it spiritually we basically think only in terms of confessing. After all, "I did it. I was wrong." Most of us miss the need for forgiveness in this instance. Who is it whom we need to forgive in such a situation? Ourselves! We have sinned and need not only God's forgiveness, but, also, a sense of our own forgiveness to prevent guilt. Very few Christians really know how to properly forgive themselves (and yet we do it the same way as in forgiving others, by an act of our will and a step of faith). Then we should reject the doubts that come into our mind that it did not work. We have done what God has said to do. We must stand in faith.

The significant hurts in us that cause us so much pain and suffering basically occur and remain because we have not understood the Biblical nature of confession and forgiveness. They are Siamese twins . . . inseparable. We must learn how to both confess and forgive if we are to be able to forget.

## FORGIVE AND FORGET

There is another principle here that is important to discern. We are forgiven so that we can forgive and forget. It is God's forgiveness of us (through confession) which in turn releases us to be able to forgive others. The combination of these two makes it possible for us to forget. God blesses us so that we may be a blessing. Remember what I said earlier. Every blessing from God comes to us on its way to someone else. It is in this circle of forgiveness that we are released from that damning memory.

If you are having trouble forgiving it is probably for one of the following reasons: (1) You have not discerned and confessed your wrong reactions, thus loosing God's forgiveness to you, or (2) you are allowing one of the three stumbling blocks* to forgiveness, as explained in the story of Billy, to get in the way. If so, re-read the story, determine the problem, and deal with it. Not to do so will only hurt you.

There is a third factor that sometimes is necessary to our being able to forget. When hurts have been buried and festering for years, the final pain and sting can sometimes only be removed with the aid of prayer visioning. Since it is the most supernatural and least understood aspect of inner healing let's look at it more closely.

### *Not Psychological Visualization*

In helping you to understand it, let me emphasize that it is not psychological visualization, even though that is what many think including some with inner healing ministries. Psychological visualization is the process of flashing mental pictures upon the screen of your imagination. The pictures as seen in the "mind's eye." It is used extensively by sales motivators, positive thinking advocates, weight watchers and many counselors. It can be psychologically beneficial through repetition and the power of suggestion, but it is not what we do in prayer visioning.

## A Vision in Prayer

Prayer visioning involves at least two spiritual gifts on the part of the inner healing counselor, word of knowledge and discernment of spirits. It is a faith action and centers around God giving a vision in prayer. A good biblical example is II Kings 6:7. Here's the backdrop. Elisha was the prophet of Israel. He and his servant lived in the city of Dothan. As the servant (Gehazi) was out "jogging" one morning he saw thousands of Syrian troops surrounding the city to try to capture Elisha. At the sight of them he becomes a "sprinter" heading straight back to Elisha with the news. He was in a frantic panic!

Elisha, like a true prophet, was cool, calm and collected. His reply to Gehazi was, "Do not fear, for those who are with us are more than those who are with them." There was no way Gehazi could understand such a statement in the light of the circumstances. (That's why we must not be limited to "sense" knowledge through our intellect. Listen to Teaching 117 on "Two Kinds of Knowledge.") So Elisha did not try to explain it to him. He simply prayed, "O Lord, open his eyes that he may see." God honored the prophet's prayer by drawing back the veil on the spiritual world and showing Gehazi thousands of angelic warriors and chariots! That's a prayer vision. It's God showing us in prayer what he's doing to meet the existing need. It is more sensed in one's spirit than seen by the mind's eye.

When people come to us with deep emotional hurts God frequently gives a prayer vision to supernaturally assist in the healing. As we counsel in the flow of the Holy Spirit, the prayer of my heart is a two-part one much like Elisha's. First, "Let them see what I see," and He does!

There is no way to understand prayer visioning intellectually. It simply is to be experienced spiritually and received emotionally. Under God's anointing, it heals the deepest hurts — rape, incest, child molestation and abuse, death, divorce, and on and on. It takes place only one time with any given hurt. Many times where there have been long repressed hurts, prayer visioning is imperative to our being able to forget once and for all. That is God's desire for us, whatever it takes — He wants us to be able to forgive and then forget!

## A HEALING PRAYER

Father, we praise you for your healing mercy. Thank you for loving and accepting us with all our hurts, hang-ups and sins, but thank you even more for caring enough to change us. Thank you for saving us from ourselves and our unwittingly self-destructive tendencies. We reach out and open up to receive your tender mercies praising you for showing us that we are forgiven so that we may be able to forgive — both ourselves and others! Amen.

*Chapter 6*

# THE RAGE OF SELF-PITY

Everyone has both anger and fear as part of their emotional make-up. We are a mix of the two. However, each of us is more prone in one direction or the other by virtue of our basic personality temperament.

In the anger-prone person, anger is a very basic personality ingredient giving motivation, aggressiveness, and competitiveness to his life. The anger-prone person is a much more driven individual and tends to have greater self-confidence than one who is fear-prone. Anger is a much more normal part of his life.

The fear-prone person tends to be much more negative, shy, and less confident. Fear causes one to withdraw and to be more readily discouraged or defeated as well as much more depression-prone. Fear-prone people have many more problems with inferiority, inadequacy, loneliness, melancholy and fears of all kinds. Anger is more foreign to their nature, and yet, it is this matter of anger in the fear-prone individual with which this chapter is concerned. It is a special kind of anger, as we shall see. Usually it is an anger that builds slowly over a long period, simmering and stewing like a pot of prunes on the back burner of one's life. Over a period of many years, it can grow from an anger which is almost imperceptible to a literal rage, rooted in self-pity.

## ANGER TO RAGE

The distance from anger to rage is a much shorter trip in the anger-prone person than in the fear-prone one. Understand what I'm saying. The anger-prone person can experience rage much more readily. It is more natural and normal than for the fear-prone person. For instance, in the anger box of the inner healing reaction chart, we would find such characteristics as resentment, bitterness, rebellion, hostility, and even rage. An anger-prone person's anger can much more rapidly accelerate and amplify to the point of rage than can a fear-prone person's. So when a fear-prone individual comes to the point of a rage in his life, it has been a much longer, slower process. For instance, if you have a child who already has anger to the point of rage in him, the odds are that the child is anger-prone by personality temperament, not fear-prone. The exception to that would be if that rage of self-pity came in fetally from one or both of the parents. This is very possible and happens on occasion, but it is not the norm. Usually the rage of self-pity is a building process.

## A Spectrum of Anger

Of course, this is modified by how much anger there is in the particular fear-prone individual, since everyone is a combination of both emotions. If one were 60% fear and 40% anger, there would be a pretty good mix of anger in them. If they are 75% fear-prone and 25% anger-prone, it would take that much longer for it to build to a rage. So, what I'm talking about is a spectrum of anger, a spectrum of anger that is rooted in self-pity. It can be anywhere from what we would normally identify as anger all the way up to a rage that can explode in violence.

For instance, I remember in August of 1966 returning to Austin, Texas, where I had previously pastored, to visit friends. I was driving along the edge of the University of Texas campus. Suddenly, I saw policemen waving me out of the way, getting me off of the street. Looking up I saw little puffs of smoke coming off the top of the tower of the University. Then, on the radio, I heard the report that there was a sniper on the tower indiscriminately shooting people. Before the afternoon had ended, seventeen people lay dead and several others had been wounded. The dead included a pregnant mother and her unborn child, all of which had died by the hand of a young man named Charles Whitman. There were many statements of disbelief that he could be responsible. "He couldn't do that. He was an Eagle Boy Scout!" 'He was such a nice, quiet young man." Deep within him though, I believe, was a growing rage of self-pity which finally exploded. If so, it had been internal long before it ever became external. This is characteristic of the fear-prone person, not the anger-prone. The anger-prone individual is much more likely to let it hang out, to express it. In a fear-prone person, that anger will smolder and build, growing slowly but gradually, moving toward rage. It will seldom reach the level which it did in Charles Whitman, but it is always harmful to the person who has it and to the people around him.

## A RAGE OF SELF-PITY

Secondly, when a fear-prone person's anger grows to the point of rage, it is pre-eminently the rage of self-pity. Now, as I've said, unless it comes in fetally, it usually will not be evident at the level of rage until that person is in their late teens or adult years. It is the cumulative effect of many experiences of rejection and hurt in one who is fear-prone. It must be preceded by anger, resentment, bitterness and rebellion. As the anger amplifies to the level of rage, it will frequently be characterized by a sudden, snarling, devouring kind of extreme anger that just leaps out emotionally, and sometimes physically. It will usually be expressed by verbal abuse — words and tone of voice, and by angrily distorted facial expressions. At times the person will realize how he is behaving, and other times he will be completely oblivious to it — even if pointed out by another.

I confess with remorse that I was one of those with this kind of rage — usually quite patient, but on certain occasions consumed by its ferocity. At this point, inner healing and seeking to walk daily in the Spirit have removed most, but not all of it. I must go deeper still in both my daily walk and my healing experience to be set completely free of it. But free I will be, for all things are possible in Christ, and what is possible for me is for you also.

Part of the problem of healing for many is the matter of recognition and confession. "It's not nice to be angry." "Good little Christians don't behave that way" — or if they do, they feverishly seek to hide it. After all, as someone has said, "Confession may be good for the soul, but it's bad for the reputation!" "Christians are nice people; they don't get mad." What foolishness! — Everybody has anger; there are no exceptions. When I talk about being angry at God, I frequently get the most sanctimonious expressions. I tell them, "Don't give me those saintly looks, like you don't understand what I'm saying. Everyone has been angry at God at some time and most still are to some degree. We're not talking about something that's terrible; we're talking about being human and that hits all of us, unless you have rigor mortis. Even small children experience anger towards God — over a divorce, the death of a parent or even of a pet. The only really terrible thing is to allow the hurt and resentment to remain buried and ignored or denied, causing devastation in our lives and the lives of the loved ones around us. This allows negative feelings to develop into wrong attitudes.

The rage within me was self-apparent long before the self-pity. People don't like the term self-pity, but all it means is feeling sorry for oneself. Who hasn't felt that way at times? We've all been mistreated at times, and some horribly so. That's why this rage of self-pity if preeminently the rage of the fear-prone person, because they allow themselves to be mistreated by others much more-readily. Some anger-prone individuals have it but it grows out of the fear aspect of their personality make-up.

## A DEFENSIVE RAGE

This rage of the fear-prone person is in its essence a defensive anger. It is the rage of a wounded or cornered animal. Its basic purpose is to protect its possessor from further mistreatment — not primarily to hurt others, but to keep us from receiving anymore hurt at the hands of others. If an anger-prone person grows to the point of rage in his anger, it will basically be an offensive rage. They strike out with the intention of hurting somebody and getting back at them, but not the fearful individual. Do you understand the difference? Rage in a fear-prone person is basically a defensive rage while rage in an anger-prone person is an offensive one. It can appear on the surface that one is trying to hurt another person is an offensive one. It can appear on the surface that one is trying to hurt another person, but the real rage of self-pity is not trying to hurt nearly so much as it is trying to protect. Back a wounded animal into a corner and it will growl and even bite, but it's not attacking. It's retreating as far as it can, and when it can't retreat any more it has to stand its ground, because at that point it's more afraid of being hurt than it is of fighting back. That's the way a fear-prone person is. A fearful individual may take it and take it and take it, but there will come a day when he becomes so angry about being mistreated or walked on, whether that mistreatment is real or imagined, that he has to fight back. At this point it is a defensive rage rooted in a deep sense of self-pity.

## It's Not Fair

Internally there is a voice crying out from our subconscious. It is saying things within us such as, "Don't treat me like that. It's not fair." "I want my way; you're cheating me out of what's rightfully mine, like so many others have." Or it may be saying, "Don't you treat me like Daddy did!" "Don't treat me like Mamma did!" "Don't you treat me like my first husband!" "You can't get away with doing me like that!" Do you understand the thrust of this kind of anger now? It is defensive; the individual has reached an emotional saturation point and he can't take any more, or he won't take it. Another thing which that internal voice is saying is "Don't remind me of the bad times with . . ." Do you catch the defensive aspect of it?

It's basically triggered only in certain situations by specific significant people. In other words, if you are a fear-prone person who has grown into this rage of self-pity, it will not normally be triggered by just anyone. It is usually triggered by only a few people, and triggered only in certain specific kinds of situations. You see, for most of us there are only a few people who can really cut us deeply. With other people it doesn't matter nearly as much. But when one of those important people in our lives pokes us where we already hurt too badly, and the emotions have layered up to the level of the rage of self-pity, we are going to explode with that rage. In my case, it was basically with my son. He was the one who could most

*Chapter 6: The Rage of Self-Pity*

easily trigger the hurt in me which was rooted in my relationship with my father. The internal voice would be saying, "I don't have to put up with it from you." Yet, it was not usually a rage that did anything physical. At times it caused me to spank him when I was angry and that was wrong, but most of the time it was a verbal abuse. Verbal, not in the sense of cursing, but of the tone of my voice and some humiliating words on occasion — mostly the angry tone of my voice and the distortion in my face. At times my son would just cower in fear because of the way I looked and sounded. Sometimes he would look like a little frightened rabbit, and that would make me angry. I genuinely thought that he was pretending, thinking I would feel sorry for him and stop. How deceived I was by the rage of self-pity that was controlling me in those moments. My heart breaks when I recall such experiences. I don't ever want to be that way again — I don't want to hurt people, even to keep from being hurt. I want to dare to be as vulnerable as Jesus was, and I want to be able to take hurt in Christ without being devastated by it and without having to strike back at people.

## *Old Testament Examples*

Let's look at some biblical examples of this rage of self-pity. A prime example is King Saul's attitude towards the young man David. David had been anointed by the prophet Samuel to succeed Saul, and the rage of self-pity within Saul greatly hastened the day of that succession. He persecuted David in many, many ways as that rage and self-pity would well up within him. The rest of the time he loved him as a son. He vacillated back and forth between the two emotions. (I Samuel 18,19). On occasion, the self-pity would be so great that he would lose all control and try to kill David himself. David innocently triggered what had been building in Saul for years. It was Saul himself who destroyed his own position of leadership by his rage of self-pity.

Another person who seemed to suffer with it was Moses. He had a deep inferiority complex which was evident in God's appearance to him in the burning bush. He told him what He wanted him to do, but it was incredulous to this desert shepherd. "You don't mean me; I couldn't do that — I don't have the ability. What would I say when I got there? ... I'd be tongue-tied." He made excuse after excuse to God, until God said, "I'll send your brother along; he's never at a loss for words. He can always say something; we'll let him be your mouthpiece."\*

Remember when Moses in anger struck the rock for water? (Numbers 20:10,11:24) It appears to have been the rage of self-pity — he felt abused and misused by the Hebrew people. "They never have really appreciated the sacrifices

I've made for them!" He had never asked for the job in the first place. He was not a status seeker. He hadn't wanted all that responsibility, and they had never been really grateful. How many times he must have gotten fed up with the way the children of Israel treated him. How they took him for granted. There were probably times when he thought that it would have been smarter for God to let the parted waters of the sea cover the Hebrews along with the Egyptians. At times the self-pity pushed him into depression and a few times it exploded into rage.

## *New Testament Example*

Judas was another prime example. Jesus didn't treat him right. He should have been part of the inner circle of the apostles. After all, he was the treasurer. Can you imagine any group today where the treasurer wouldn't be part of the inner circle — but Judas was excluded. Judas wanted Jesus to be a different kind of Messiah than He was. He felt mistreated because Jesus wasn't doing it right. Now, I can identify with Judas. I used to tell God that He was missing the boat all the time. "God, don't you know what's going on? Sometimes you act like you don't know which end is up!" That's how I know God is a merciful God. I wouldn't be here now if He weren't! Some of you fall into the same category. You've talked to God like that. Judas was like that, too. Why did he take his life? I believe it was because he was in a rage of self-pity. He took a calculated risk. He wanted Jesus to stand up to the Romans and fight. He thought if they attempted to take Jesus captive that He would have to fight them. He wouldn't let them take Him prisoner. Everyone would rally to Jesus and overthrow the Romans, but that wasn't what happened, and when Judas realized that his plans had failed, he went out and killed himself in a rage of self-pity (Matthew 27:5).

## **INTERNAL AND EXTERNAL**

There is a fourth basic factor which we need to realize. The rage of self-pity has two aspects: internal and external. Everyone who has the rage of self-pity has it internally; there are no exceptions. If you don't have it internally, you don't have it at all. All emotional problems begin internally, not externally. What is on the outside is indicative of what's on the inside. Most people with this rage of self-pity have it in both areas.

There are a few people for whom it seems to be only internal. They don't appear to explode in any kind of rage on the outside. I know that this can be so with children and youth, and perhaps even with young adults. When an individual has it only internally, the person does not blow up outwardly, and it is much more difficult to detect. The self-pity aspect is easier to discern in this instance than the rage. When it is only internal, the rage aspect can refer to two things: the internal intensity of the emotional feelings and the fury with which the internal rage fights to maintain its emotional and spiritual stronghold in one's life — albeit an undetected one.

## *Spiritual Warfare*

It is important that we realize that this internal battle is both emotional and spiritual. We are in a war, but it is not simply human warfare. As it says in II Corinthians 10:3,4: "For though we walk in the flesh, we do not war after the flesh: For the weapons of our warfare are not carnal, but mighty through God to the pulling down of strongholds." (KJV) This rage of self-pity is always both an emotional and a demonic problem. Realize that Christians are not demon possessed*, but Christians have many problems in the area of spiritual warfare. This is so because evil spirits are simply Satan's army and he uses his army primarily against God's people. The spirits do not originate or cause problems in the lives of Christians; they infiltrate through the open doors which our unconfessed sins and emotional wounds give them — seeking to establish spiritual and emotional strongholds in the believer's life, compounding and amplifying every problem. A stronghold is simply a strong hold spiritually and emotionally which the enemy is able to obtain in a given area of our life. To the degree that it is a stronghold, to that degree it has become a compulsive area in our life and we no longer have free willful control over it.

There are no perfect people without any problems at all. All of us have areas yet to be yielded to the Lord. Christians are still under construction and always will be. We don't have to be perfect because Jesus is perfect, and He paid the penalty for our sins in full. We all have hurts, hang-ups and some unconfessed sin. We must come to grips with the negative emotional factors in our lives. Fear of making possible negative confessions brought back to mind by Satan is not nearly the problem that. Spiritual deception is. Denying the reality of internal newels, whether emotional or spiritual, is a self-defeating process. We each have negatives within us as believers with God's Spirit will resurface periodically and which must be dealt with as from God. I John 1:8 which was written to believers makes this quite clear.

When we fail to deal with what God is seeking to reveal, we are saying "no" to Him and punishing ourselves. Unable, then, to release these pressure points (spiritually and emotionally) the internal stress within us will grow and grow, becoming like the engine of a fast racing car — idling too fast and increasing the deadly stress within us. Like a teapot on the stove, it must eventually cool down or blow — there are no other alternatives.

## Strong Self-Rejection

It is also important for us to realize that this rage of self-pity is usually allied with a strong sense of self-rejection. The person who has the rage of self-pity tends to set himself up for rejection. Ever wonder why you experience so much rejection? We set ourselves up for years. I didn't realize it at the time, but I did. There are many things which could be touched upon at this time as to how we set ourselves up, but let me mention one in particular. It is unrealistic expectations. We all have some unrealistic expectations that can never be met with any consistency or frequency, and every time they are not we feel rejected all over again. Each of us has them — where are yours? Where are you setting yourself up for — rejection with unrealistic expectations? In your marriage? With your children? In your job? Spiritually, because Of unbalanced teaching on prosperity or healing? Financially by over-extending your credit? Sometimes we know we'll be rejected in a given type of situation and still ourselves up for it to happen. When I say we know it, I'm not talking so much about knowing it consciously, as subconsciously and emotionally.

## Unrealistic Expectations

Let me give you an illustration that comes to mind. When my son was three or four years old, I'd say, "Son, I love you," and sometimes he'd say "Daddy, I love you," and throw his arms around my neck and hug me. That was worth a million dollars! But there are times when you tell a three-year-old that you love him and his mind is two blocks away by the time you get the word "you" out! So he wouldn't even hear me. He wasn't rejecting me; he was just being a three-year-old. It isn't a realistic expectation to expect a three-year-old to respond verbally in the way an adult might. But I had an unrealistic expectation because I had an inordinate need. My real need was to hear my dad say that he loved me.

My son's silence in those instances painfully reminded me of my daddy's silence in the same area when I was a child. Literally his doing and saying nothing would trigger hurting memories and cause me to react in self-pity. He would turn and see my face and say, "What's wrong, Daddy?" I would angrily retort, "Nothing!" Then my face would contort a little more, and he'd say, "What did I do, Daddy?" "You didn't do anything, now leave me alone!" What was he doing to trigger me? First of all, I was setting myself up for rejection with an unrealistic expectation. That's not how one relates to a three-year-old, because they don't verbalize their love on demand. They tend to do it more spontaneously. It comes or it doesn't come, and one might as well accept that as part of the way a three-year-old is. Secondly, as I said, he was triggering my rejection with his silence. Because, you see, that's what I felt all of my life. It seemed that every time I needed to hear my daddy say that he loved me, there was just silence. I can never remember hearing him say he loved me, even though I realize now that he did.

It became the same way with my wife; I could never hear her say she loved me enough. I set myself up for rejection. I finally realized that she could have told me all the time, and it wouldn't have convinced me because I was expecting a person to do what only God can do. People can't love us retroactively. They can't go back and fill in the vacuum that's been there for years. Only God can do that. People loving us the best they can love us still doesn't do much about that lack of love in the past. Much of the need will remain. When a woman comes into a marriage relationship expecting both the love of a husband and the love of a father, she has an unrealistic expectation that can never be met. If he were a perfect husband and gave her 100% of everything that he could give her (and there aren't any like that), he might only give her half of what she needed. When a man comes into a marriage needing both the love of a wife and a mother, he can never get all that he needs from his wife. God has to go back in there and give that retroactive love Himself; and that's what inner healing is. Jesus goes back into the memory and fills the void which, in its essence, is a lack of love.

## *Failure to Communicate*

Rejection stems from not feeling loved, accepted, affirmed, and/or approved with the people we need, when we need it, and in the way we need it. It is not basically a problem of people not loving us, as much as it is a problem of not effectively communicating our love to each other. I realize now that was my dad's problem. He loved me, but had difficulty communicating it to me. With whom do we have the most trouble communicating it? The people we love the most. They are the ones who can trigger emotions and hurt us the easiest, and the ones with whom it is most difficult to communicate what we really feel, because they are so important to us. If we have any fear of commitment or failure or confrontation, let alone fear of rejection, which is always there in some degree, it is difficult for us to allow ourselves to be vulnerable enough to deeply give and receive love. Thus, our love factor is out of balance and the whole key to life is this matter of balance.

Anger is not necessarily wrong, but anger out of balance can become rage. Being self-protective is not wrong, but self-pity is self-protection out of balance. The devil doesn't care whether we're in left field or right field, as long as we're not in center field. He just wants us out of balance; that's all it takes to prevent Jesus being able to give us an abundant life as He desires (John 10:10). This unbalance permits anger to be triggered in us before the other person has actually said or done anything, simply by our anticipation of their rejection.

## Reacting to Anticipations

I remember an illustration which I think is a classic. I heard Dr. Bill Bright tell it many years ago. A man was driving down a dark country road about two o'clock in the morning. A tire blew out, so he got out and went to the trunk of the car only to find he had no jack! No jack at two o'clock in the morning, in the middle of nowhere with a flat tire! He was already exhausted, and he had no jack. This is what is known as frustration. In his frustration and aggravation, he saw a farmhouse off in the distance, maybe a half mile away. He knew the only thing he could possibly have done was to walk to that farmhouse and wake those people to ask them if he could borrow their jack. So he started walking. Now, this was a fear-prone man who had the rage of self-pity in him. As he walked he began to think about what was going to happen when he knocked on that door at nearly three o'clock in the morning, waking that man out of a sound sleep. He was a total stranger. He knew the farmer was going to be mad. He just knew that he was going to be upset and angry at being awakened; this man began to react to this anticipated response before he even reached the house. He finally arrived and knocked on the door. The window went up above the door, and the farmer stuck his head out and said, "Howdy, neighbor, how can I help you?" And the man exploded, "Keep your blankety-blank old jack; I didn't want it anyway!"

Now, what did he do? He reacted in a rage of self-pity by simply anticipating what he thought the farmer was going to do. Have you ever done that? Have you ever reacted because of your anticipation of what you thought would happen? Such as not wanting to make a phone call, because you just know what they are going to say, so you try to avoid it. There have been some phone calls that I never made, but I was so mad over what I thought they would have said if I had called them that I could justify never having made the call! You know the feeling. Sometimes it is difficult to discern what triggers the rage of self-pity in us. It can range anywhere from something very obvious to seemingly nothing. Literally silence can trigger it, or our anticipation of what that silence means. It is hard to pinpoint and discern the trigger until we begin to develop some real sensitivity to where we are coming from emotionally. That discernment is the beginning of the road to freedom! And I believe that it is the road to the abundant life about which Jesus taught.

We blame God for not giving us the abundant life. He promised it; why doesn't he deliver? Why is there so much difference between what He promises and what I experience on a daily basis? The problem is not on God's end — it is on the human end and that includes a lot more people than just you or me. However, the only part we are really responsible for is ourselves. Within the area of our self-responsibility lies the matter of our false presumptions and prejudices. Prejudice is simply prejudgment. That man walking down the road to the farmhouse to borrow the jack was prejudging the farmer. Why? Because he had probably been in so many other situations where he was in need and when he reached out, the person didn't help him.

## *Setting Ourselves Up*

A situation comes to my mind that happened twenty five years ago. I was a youth director in a church and was fairly well-known in the area in my denomination's youth groups. We were at a youth encampment and I was one of the leaders there. The director of the camp was my ex-pastor. I pretty well had the run of everything because of his position and our relationship. One night I was talking to another of the counselors as we were out walking.

It was about midnight and we were helping to patrol the camp to make sure that all the boys were in their cabins. We were thirsty and he said, "I wish the concession stand were open so we could get something to drink." I said, "That's okay; they don't lock the window; we'll crawl in and get a pop, and I'll leave the money on the counter. I'll tell my pastor about it in the morning." So we crawled through the window, not knowing there were some other counselors patrolling the grounds, too. We crawled in, got our pop, and were coming out the window when several persons converged on us! They grabbed us like we'd committed the crime of the century, practically dragging us outside.

I thought, "What in the world?" The one area of my life that I felt was totally above reproach was my honesty and integrity. It never occurred to me that somebody could think I'd do something dishonest. I was one of those Abraham Lincoln types. If I went somewhere and they gave me a penny too much change, I might drive thirty minutes across town to return the penny. It was simply unbelievable to me that we were being accused of dishonesty.

When I talked to the camp pastor, who was a friend of mine, and I explained to him, he understood and said, "But I know how it looked, Jon, to other people who saw it." Through his talking to me I began to see that. So I went to the cabin of the counselor and the boys who had "caught" us. It was dark in the cabin as we went in to apologize. The seriousness of what they thought we had done was just beginning to grow in me. Here I was a well-known young minister and they thought I was dishonest. Satan was trying to destroy my witness.

I was weeping as I asked them to please forgive me. The boys all did so very readily, but not the man. The sound of his voice cut the darkness like a knife as he said, emphatically, "No, I won't forgive you. You don't deserve to be forgiven!" I know now that we set ourselves up for rejection, but I didn't realize that then, and his rejection of me was devastating.

God wants us to realize that we often set ourselves up for rejection and, at times, even anticipate it. We know it is coming, and we begin to react in advance. Frequently we will begin to reject ourselves in anticipation of others rejecting us. Like the man going for the jack. We don't even have to have his rejection; we've already begun the process of self-rejection, and our rage of self-pity is being triggered.

## *Rebellion and Self-Pity*

Two more factors which are closely related to the rage of self-pity are rebellion and self-deception. Let's look at self-deception for a moment. If we have that rage of self-pity, where are we most likely to be self-deceived? We are self-deceived, first of all in that many times we don't even know we have self-pity. I am amazed sometimes when I tell someone who's obviously in self-pity that he has no realization of his self-pity at all. We're frequently deceived. We can also be easily deceived at the point of our rage. Many are unaware that they have any rage at all. They are blinded to it by a spirit of self-deception. Other times they do recognize it and are self-deceived into overwhelming guilt. Again, it is the matter of balance. Satan wants to keep us out of center field, so if he can't deceive us into thinking that we don't really have a problem, he will switch to the other extreme and attack with guilt and self-condemnation.

We can also be deceived at the point of our rebellion, not realizing that we are in rebellion. Now, where are we likely to be in rebellion? Towards those who trigger us the most, and when those people who trigger us happen to be in authority over us, it multiplies the rebellion. It becomes an even more acute problem with a child or youth, because their rebellion usually is related to parents, and they are in authority over them. We can also be in rebellion towards those of whom we are jealous or envious. Many times in our self-pity we feel treated so unfairly that it looks like someone else is really being treated much better than we are. "I don't deserve that. I don't deserve to be treated less fairly than they." That creates sibling rivalry. But it can create rivalry in any area when we tend to be envious or jealous of others.

A common way that this is expressed in fear-prone people is in wishing they were someone else. Have you ever wished that your hair was like someone else's, or that you lived where they live, or that your nose was like their nose? I remember a lovely young woman I ministered to several years ago. There had been some real demonic problems. I had bound them, and she was changing and opening up. God began to tell me some things about her. I said, "God just told me you don't like your nose." She said, "I hate my nose! I hate my nose!" She was a beautiful girl, so why did she hate her nose? Because her older sister was very petite and she, by comparison, was larger. Then I said, "God just told me you hate your hands." "Oh, my hands are so big they look like a man's hands! And I hate my feet; I can't stand my feet!" I said, "Why do you hate your feet?" She said, "Because they are so big and ugly." They weren't really big, but her sister's were smaller so she felt big in comparison.

## *Envy Creates Self-Rejection*

Much of our self-rejection grows out of our envy of other people. The odd thing is that they are often envious of us at the same time. One afternoon I was teaching a women's group in another state. After the meeting one woman told me that she had been envious of another lady across the room. She said, "She is so attractive, and as she talked about the good things in her life, I felt so jealous… until she happened to mention that she was separated from her seventh husband!" She said, "I was eaten up with self-pity until I heard that, and I thought about the fact that I'm still with my first one and it's pretty good." The other woman would have been envious of her!

That's the way envy is; it doesn't know all the facts. The grass always looks greener on the other side of the fence until we cross over, and then it looks greener somewhere else. There really isn't basically that much difference from pasture to pasture! We just think there is because we're envious. If we could know that in advance, by foresight rather than hindsight, it would prevent a lot of problems.

## A KEY TO DEPRESSION

Let me say one final thing, as my sixth major point in this chapter. Understanding the rage of self-pity is a significant key to unlocking the door of depression.

Understanding this rage releases the grip that depression has on one's life. As I've said in my teachings on depression, that depression begins with a disappointment (or rejection) and always involves self-pity; it locks us into continuing or chronic depression. Its intensity may fluctuate, but I doubt that we can ever be completely out of it. One can function fairly well in many areas of life and still be in mild chronic depression.

As I have come to understand the rage of self-pity in relationship to depression, I can see why so many psychiatrists feel that anger is perhaps the most basic factor in depression. When a psychiatrist encounters the person in deep depression, they see the rage of self-pity and identify it as anger. This then seems to substantiate anger as prime cause of depression and it is, but not in the psychological sense that many think. Fear is still much more basic because the anger-prone person can never go as deep into depression as the fear-prone individual. Anger motivates a person and causes him to strike back, even as he is entering into depression. The fear-prone person tends to just give in, and give up — that's why the fear-prone person frequently will tend to want to sleep more and feel fatigued, because he is retreating like a turtle drawing its head back into its shell.

## *God-Given Dreams*

Let me say one other important thing about depression. One cannot be in deep depression or remain in continuing depression without having lost his dreams — the dreams that God implants inside us. We must never stop having those God-given dreams. They give purpose and motivation on a deep level. One of the critical things that must be done with depression-prone people is to rebuild and restore those God-given dreams. They are the real goals and purpose(s) to motivate our life. Not materialistic dreams; psychologists try that. Materialism often doesn't motivate really fear-prone people anyway; they frequently don't feel any real ability to accomplish materialistic things — but our God-given dreams give us a real reason for living and fighting back. Tune in and find out what those dreams are that God has implanted in you but that have almost died out. Find them and fan them back to flame again. (One of the difficulties at times in helping them do this is the problem of overmedication which can prevent them from hearing the voice of their spirit.)

## *Know Your Wrong Thoughts*

The warmth and glow of those dreams can help put out the rage of self-pity. When we give up and give in, we lose our dreams and go deeper and deeper into self-pity. Let me say to you as strongly as I know how: self-pity is an absolute "NO, NO!" It is totally wrong. It is a completely wrong thought. You must learn what your wrong thoughts are. We each have a handful of "wrong thoughts" which tend to keep us in self-defeat. Guilt is always a wrong thought. Fear is always a wrong thought. Self-pity is always a wrong thought. You must come to grips with those thoughts and use the "Five Steps to Victory in Your Thought Life"* to overcome them. Recognize and reject those wrong thoughts. They are wrong for you because they are bad for you. They are bad for you because they are self-defeating, self-destructive, and counter-productive. Guilt never helps you. Self-pity never helps. Fear never helps. They are "NO, NO's!"

Begin to see these thoughts as luxuries you cannot afford, as I had to do. They cost too much. Thoughts of suicide are a luxury I cannot afford. It almost destroyed me on several occasions. You will never get well — you will never be free of depression as long as you leave open the door to suicide as an option in your life. You must close the door. You must determine, "I have options, but that's not one of them." As long as you leave the door cracked, it'll keep trying to suck you back into it until it takes your life. Guilt is the same way. I would react in a rage of self-pity and then take a guilt trip. That didn't solve anything. Guilt is a put-down feeling, and God doesn't want us to put ourselves down.

## *Love Yourself!*

He wants you to come to understand yourself so you can see yourself like He sees you and begin to love yourself that way. The second greatest love affair in anyone's life ought to be with themselves. Our first and greatest love affair must be with Jesus Christ, but the second is to be with yourself, or you're not in Biblical balance. In Luke 10:27 Jesus shows us the two greatest commandments. "You shall love the Lord your God with all your heart, and with all your soul, and with all your strength, and with all your mind; and your neighbor as yourself." Perhaps you've heard of the J-O-Y acrostic: J-esus first, O-thers second, Y-ourself third. It sounds so noble, but it's not. It is unbiblical. You can only love others the way God wants you to, to the degree that you can recognize and receive His love for you. You must come to love yourself the way God loves you. The JOY acrostic is a distortion of man. It sounds so Christ-like, but it is not.

Why did Jesus forgive people? He did not preeminently forgive people for their sake. He first and foremost forgave people for His sake. Do you understand that? It was in His best self-interest to forgive others. Why? He knew if He did not forgive them, then a spirit of unforgiveness would develop and back up in Him and poison His system like ours have been poisoned. Then, He, too, would be guilty of sin, and it would abort His whole mission for coming to earth. He had to forgive; He didn't forgive because people came and asked Him. Nowhere in the New Testament is it ever recorded that anyone told Jesus they were sorry and asked His personal forgiveness. Not one time, and yet He always forgave them. Why? He forgave them primarily for His benefit, not because they deserved it. Many will not deserve it, so don't get hung up on that. If we want to get technical, none of us deserve most of the forgiveness we receive. God doesn't forgive us because we deserve it; He forgives us because He loves us and because it is part of His nature. If we are like Jesus and have the nature of God, we will forgive. However, if we remain hung up on all the little things, it will merely feed our self-pity until it becomes like a raging inferno inside of us.

## 3 Reasons for My Freedom

Whom will it destroy? Oh, it will destroy and hurt those around us, especially the ones we love the most, but pre-eminently it will destroy us. It is a self-destructive process. It will prevent our lives from achieving their maximum potential. Too many go through life feeling, "Ah, what might have been." Several years ago I heard Keith Miller say, "So many people go through life always in dress rehearsal, never getting to the real thing." And I said, "Oh, God, all my life has been a dress rehearsal; I'm tired of being in dress rehearsal!" It was two more years before I began to feel like I was finally on the stage of life doing some of the things I ought to have been doing. I spent six months of that two years on the verge of suicide, but He brought me out of it, and He's kept me out of it for three reasons. I've shared them before, and I'll share them over and over with every breath in me. First, because of the inner healing He has done within me. Second, because of the principles He's taught me from His Word which I'm sharing here with you. Third, by my practicing those principles. If you don't practice them, it doesn't matter what they are.

When someone tells me that my teachings are repetitious, I know one thing. They're not really hearing what's on them. Certainly they are repetitious, even as the Word of God is repetitious, but they reverberate with life-giving principles. They are rooted in God's Word and when they really get down inside of you, they will transform your life! They contain the depth and wisdom of God which He has taught me and by which He has transformed my life. He can and will yours, too, if you'll dare to pay the price of these three steps I've just mentioned.

*Chapter 6: The Rage of Self-Pity*

## *I've Been There!*

I have been where you may be right now as you read this book. I've been in the hell of depression. I've been on the verge of suicide. I've been suffocated with guilt. I've reeked with self-pity. I was devastated by rejection and the fear of it for years, but never again. Jesus Christ has set me free, and I yearn for that same freedom for you. I want it for you and each of those whom your life touches.

As far as I am concerned, it is not an accident that you are reading those words. It is a divine appointment between you and God. He loves you and He wants to set you free, more than you will ever know or understand. Jesus came to "set the captives free!" He has me, and He will you. But you must get off of the pity-party. The problem isn't on God's end — the problem is on the human end. Don't take a guilt trip with that statement; the "human end" doesn't mean simply you. There are many people who have had input into your life. There are many people who have affected you and infected you. Every significant person in your life has contributed to who you are.

## *Your Own Responsibility*

If we were to measure your responsibility for what you do and have done with your life on a scale from one to one hundred, it would be something like this: your personal responsibility ranges in the area of 25-35%; your parents and immediate family into whose world you came would measure another 25-30-35% of the responsibility; if you round both of those off to 30% each, you still have 40% left; that belongs to the other significant people who have had an impact on your life and to society in general. What is it that overwhelms and devastates us? It is when we feel like we're 80, 90 or 100% responsible for the mess we're in. God never said we're totally responsible — man says that. We're born with a sin nature, and we come into a sin-filled society. But God will never tell us that we have no responsibility either. It isn't the 30% of the responsibility that devastates us; it's the sense that we are totally responsible which overwhelms and defeats us. If I were counseling with you, I wouldn't allow you to take a guilt trip for that other 70%, but I would hold your feet to the fire on facing up to the responsibility of that 30%! That's where your healing lies. You'll never be healed by dwelling on what somebody did to you. You'll only be healed by coming to grips with your wrong reactions, confessing them to the Lord, receiving His forgiveness, and forgiving them. Then you can allow Jesus to do whatever He has to do to put the icing on the cake, to bring it all together in what we call prayer visioning. He wants to heal you and set you free in Christ!

*Chapter 7*

# DEFEATING DEPRESSION

Depression is as old as mankind and the Bible is replete with examples of it, even in its greatest saints. They've included Abraham, Moses, David, and Peter. Psalm 42:5 is a good example. "Why are you in despair, O my soul, and why have you become disturbed within me?" The psalmist is talking to himself saying, "Why do I hurt so much? Why do I feel this way? What is it within me that creates the confusion and indecision, the turmoil in my mind and in my soul?" Have you ever had this kind of conversation with yourself? Multiplied millions have at one time or another.

In Psalm 139:12 David affirms that "even the darkness is not dark to thee." I know of no deeper darkness than the darkness of depression and the loneliness and sadness that comes with it so many times. The psalmist is saying, "It doesn't matter how dark things are or how dark they seem, even the darkness is not dark to God." He can see through our darkness, sort out the confusion, and meet our needs where we are.

One of the most moving scriptures is Psalm 142:7: "Bring my soul out of prison so that I may give thanks to thy name." When our soul, or mind, is imprisoned by our hurts and problems, it is hard to praise God. The psalmist cries out, as we sometimes must, "Bring my soul out of prison so I can really praise you, Father!" Certainly part of coming out of that prison within ourselves is learning to praise God in ALL things, even in the midst of the darkness. This is vital! When we are set free, then we can praise Him in a way that we are never able to do otherwise.

Another tremendously positive passage is Jeremiah 29:11, "For I know the plans that I have for you, declares the Lord. Plans for welfare and not for calamity, to give you a future and a hope." That is what God wants for us! Jesus said, "I am come that you might have life and have it more abundantly." God wants to give us that fullness of life. The word "abundant" in the original Greek means "over-flowing, or running over." That's the kind of life God wants for us.

There is another verse of scripture that has been special to me for over twenty years. It is Luke 4:18. Jesus was at the synagogue in His hometown of Nazareth. Having been asked to be the guest teacher, He opened the scripture and read from Isaiah 61. Then He said to them, "Today, this scripture has been fulfilled in your hearing" (Luke 4:21). This was a passage that pointed to the Messiah and described His ministry. Jesus said, "The Spirit of the Lord is upon me, because he hath anointed me to preach the gospel to the poor; he hath sent me to heal the broken-hearted, to preach deliverance to the captives, and recovering of sight to the blind, to set at liberty them that are bruised" (KJV). This was Jesus' ministry then, and it is now. God is still in the business of setting the prisoner free, giving sight to the blind and releasing the captive! This is no less so in the emotional area than it is in the physical, spiritual, or financial area. Whatever our need, God wants to meet it. Wherever we hurt, God wants to heal us. Whatever the lack, God wants to fill it. It sometimes takes a while to begin to realize this and to accept it, but it is so. God wants more for us than we ever dare to dream.

## A UNIVERSAL PROBLEM

Depression is a universal problem. Has anyone ever lived who has not experienced it to some degree at some time? Some live with it continually and are chronically depressed. Suicide has now become the Number 2 killer in America and its greatest cause is depression. People become depressed, weary of living, and consider life simply an existence. They no longer care to exist on such a level and end their life. Many who have studied in this area believe that depression causes more human suffering than any other disease known to man. I agree. It is so prevalent and at times can be like a living hell. God no more wants His people in hell on this earth than in the world to come.

Most counselors would acknowledge that there are three stages to depression: mild, serious, and severe. I prefer to identify these three stages as discouragement, despondency, and despair. The third stage of despair can become so severe that people lose complete contact with reality.

Depression affects us physically, emotionally, and spiritually. It is detrimental to us in each of these three basic areas. Symptoms are many and varied: one of the most common in insecurity; continuing sadness and loneliness are prevalent; and erratic sleep patterns (either difficulty in sleeping or sleeping too much) can be symptomatic. Some to whom I have ministered wake up three and four times during the night and can only sleep in short shifts. Others who are depressed want to sleep all the time and withdraw into sleep as an escape. Additional symptoms include lethargy, apathy, and the "blahs." An excessive appetite, or the loss of it, can indicate depression — not only loss of physical appetite for food but loss of sexual appetite as well. Depression frequently leads to frigidity or impotence.

Many also lose pride in their personal appearance and don't really care how they look. Hostility, irritability, anxiety, fear, hopelessness, and hypochondria all can be symptomatic of depression. It strikes almost everyone to some degree at some time in their life.

## *Traditional Treatment*

Traditionally, depression has been dealt with in various ways. It has been treated by psychiatrists, psychologists, ministers, and counselors of various descriptions and by medical doctors. If it is depression in the mild stage, it is usually treated with counseling. But even depression in the mild stage many times can require numerous sessions from a traditional standpoint to bring any real release. If it moves into the more severe kind of depression, usually a combination of medication and psychotherapy is utilized. Perhaps the most popular kind of medication today is the so-called try-cyclic anti-depressants. Sometimes a combination of several drugs will be employed. Different drugs will work for different people. Medication is tremendously helpful to a lot of people on a short term basis, but it can create all kinds of problems if a person has to continue using it indefinitely. I remember a woman I pastored some years ago. She had gone to her gynecologist with symptoms of mild depression, so he put her on a tranquilizer. She remained on them for over four years, became addicted and abusive of the medication. She began falling and hurting herself so severely that her husband hospitalized her. They placed her in the psychiatric ward because of her addiction to the medication and she was in for thirty days going through withdrawal. Upon her release from the hospital and from the drugs, she was still depressed. It had just been masked and covered by the drugs. I'm not putting drugs down, but I am saying that they are seldom a long term answer. In addition to these methods of treatment, electric shock is still used with varying degrees of success.

## CAUSES OF DEPRESSION

Let's focus now on some of the causes of depression. The traditional and/or psychiatric perspective is that depression has many different causes. Almost any psychiatrist or clinical psychologist would say that depression is a very complex thing, emanating from many different sources. Let me share some of the things which they believe to be primary causes of depression. One is unrealistic expectations. We expect too much and we're disappointed when it does not happen, or we fail to accomplish what we had anticipated. Low self-image or self-esteem is also considered to be a primary cause of depression. It is very prevalent and can repeatedly set one up for disappointment and defeat. Physical illness can trigger depression. Post-partum depression can occur as a new mother's body metabolism is adjusting from the nine months of pregnancy. Much change is taking place in her system. Sometimes it is triggered by the fact that there is an emotional let-down after the baby has arrived. Now she is awakened at night, hanging dirty diapers and feeding the baby. If her husband is getting all of his sleep and part of hers, too, that can trigger depression!

## *Significant Loss*

A significant loss in our life (the death of a loved one, a divorce, or the loss of a child) can lead to depression. Another cause in many people is a sense of being trapped by adverse circumstances over which they have no control. Who hasn't felt that way at some time? When we come to understand what we possess in Christ, we don't have to settle for that, but few Christians really know who they are in Christ. Few really understand what it means to be a joint heir with Jesus. As we learn this, it helps put emotional control back into our hands (see Teachings 122 and 123 on Position in Christ).

## *Personality Temperament*

Another area that influences depression is the personality temperament with which one is born. Certain of the personality temperament types are depression-prone or have more of a tendency in that direction. This must be taken into consideration in determining the source of depression. The beautiful thing is that the fruit of God's Spirit can correct or compensate for any weakness in our natural temperament. Thus, it is important to learn how to be filled and walk in the Spirit, so that we can allow God to bear the fruit of His Spirit in our lives.

## *The Sin Factor*

Something else that can certainly bring on depression but would not usually be talked about in psychiatric circles is sin. Sin can produce guilt, and guilt can trigger depression. Part of the compounding problem is that guilt can be real or false. We can feel guilty when we're not, and false guilt can do the same thing as real guilt. Guilt has been defined in various ways. Psychologists sometimes speak of both the positive and negative aspects of guilt, but I believe most people think of guilt in only negative terms. When most of us are talking about guilt, what do we mean? A "put down" feeling, that feeling of being beaten down, pounded into the ground and defeated. This kind of guilt is always from our adversary, the devil, working in conjunction with our negative emotions, thought processes, and distorted imaginations.

God does not give us guilt trips — the Holy Spirit has come only to convict us. The word "convict" literally means to convince us. He is trying to convince us that what He is saying to us is right. What He says to us through His written Word is right. What His Holy Spirit says to our spirit is right. The word "confess' biblically means to "agree with God." He wants us to learn to agree with Him that whatever He is saying to us is right. He never gives us wrong advice. As we realize this, we need to line up with what He is saying to us, both through His Word (the Bible) and the inner voice of our spirit.

## REJECTION IS THE ROOT

There are many other factors that have traditionally been considered the causal factors in depression which could be considered. However, let me state my deep personal convictions at this point. First of all, I believe that only a relatively small percentage of depression can be attributed to purely physiological factors. Aside from those instances, I believe that it begins emotionally with a disappointment. In this sense disappointment is just another word for rejection. Thus, *I* believe that almost all depression begins with an experience(s) of rejection* If it is not dealt with and released in the way that God provides for and is allowed to layer up through repeated repression, then this disappointment will grow into discouragement. If the cycle is not broken here, then discouragement can grow into despondency. This cycle when allowed to continue will at times deepen into despair. One of the things I frequently do when someone comes in who is depressed is to ask how long he has been in that condition. A woman comes to mind who had been depressed a little over three months. I said, "Can you tell me what happened a little over three months ago that deeply disappointed you?" She shared two things in her relationship to her husband, and in less than an hour the depression was broken (we simply applied the three basic steps to inner healing). It is not always that easy, but many times it is.

As I expressed in the previous chapter, it is my conviction that depression always involves self-pity. Few depressed people want to hear that, but it is important to their release. We must learn to recognize and prevent our "pity parties." Most have them at one time or another. Some have them constantly. They are totally self-defeating and counter-productive. They short-circuit all that God wants to do in our lives.

## COST OF DEPRESSION

Another major aspect I want to discuss with you is the cost of depression. What is the cost, first of all, to the person who has it, the sufferer? Many times it is deep personal agony. It can be hell — a living hell. Several years ago I experienced depression to the degree that for six months I walked daily on the edge of suicide. The only thing that kept me alive, preventing me from taking my life, was the fact that I had a life insurance policy which was only a year and a half old. It would have been voided by suicide prior to its second year. I lived in daily hell for six months trying to survive until my insurance policy was two years old, so that when I took my life, I would not leave my family penniless. That would have been total failure. God raised up people to pray for me in this city and in other places. I didn't know that at the time, and they didn't know what they were praying for, but they were faithful and I am alive today. I've met five or six of those people who have shared how they interceded in my behalf, and God has allowed me, in turn, to minister to them. How I praise Him for that! I wouldn't be alive today if people hadn't listened to God and prayed for Jon Eargle! (So when God lays someone on your heart, don't lay it aside lightly. It may literally save someone's life as it did mine!) By the end of that six months, I just barely didn't want to die any more. I had written letters to my wife, son, and daughter, explaining why I had taken my life. I had written and rewritten them. I knew that hell and agony, but I don't know it any more! I never will know it again, because Jesus has healed the hurts that allowed it to happen and set me free from them. Now I relish little things about life that I never even noticed before.

I learned to rejoice in the experience I went through, not happy that I had it, but grateful that Jesus could use it to allow me to identify much more deeply with others who have been there. I am a living testimony to what God will do, how He can redeem each situation, including the terrible sadness and loneliness of depression. If you haven't experienced it, it is impossible to understand; it can be utter desolation. I don't know any other word to explain it but desolation, that abject hopelessness that can come with depression — helplessness, indecision, confusion, negativism, anxiety, a lessened ability to function. It is terribly damaging and destructive to self-esteem and can create awful embarrassment and humiliation. Many times it creates a loss of work and income, which compounds into all kinds of financial problems. Depression can carry a very high price tag — even death.

### *Hurts Those You Love*

In addition to the person who is going through it, it also hurts the family of that person. How can I know the hell through which I put my wife while depressed?

— only she and God know that. When we are depressed, our self-pity causes us to be emotionally self-centered to the point of not realizing how we are hurting those around us. I thought my love of them was the only thing that kept my alive. I loved them enough that I didn't want to die without leaving that insurance, but how many unloving things I must have done about which my wife, in her deep love for me, never said anything. What devastation it often causes family members. As the song says, "We always hurt the ones we love, the ones we shouldn't hurt at all." When we are really depressed, it is almost impossible to respond in a normal way and we react more and more, hurting the very ones we love most.

## CURE FOR DEPRESSION

It thrills me to be able to say that there is a cure for depression. No one has to remain in depression indefinitely. The cure comes much more easily sometimes than it does other times, but God has a cure and wants us to know that. I guarantee you, no matter how long it takes, it is worth it! It is worth it because life can be richer, fuller and more meaningful than you have ever dreamed. What is the cure for depression? Let me give you the answer in two words, and then let me tell you how you can experience that and cooperate with it. The answer is agape love. God's unconditional love for us. There is no hurt in our lives that God's love will not heal.

When we are in depression, one thing is certain. We do not know how much God loves us. I think there is invariably anger towards God as well as towards people who rejected us because when we hurt, we really don't feel as though God cares. You know the feeling, "If God really cared, He wouldn't leave me in this mess. If He were really concerned about me, He wouldn't let me hurt like this." This feeling is usually perceived as rejection from God and eventually produces anger at Him. Can you recognize that you have anger at God inside of you, at least on a subconscious level? There isn't anyone who hasn't been angry at God sometimes, but some Christians have great difficulty acknowledging it! Others find it such a relief to be able to say, "Yes, I'm mad at Him!" and I say, "That's great!" He already knows it. He just Wants us to realize it and confess it. I used to correct God, update Him, explain things to Him and tell Him what He didn't seem to understand. He's got to be a loving God to ever put up with that!

# 8 STEPS TO VICTORY

Let me share with you eight steps for preventing depression in your life, and in the course of this I'll also talk about how to break depression.

## *Born Again and Filled*

1. The first necessity in preventing depression is A SPIRITUAL REBIRTH. You must be born again* (John 3:3, 16-18). It means that you must come to that point in your life when you accept Jesus Christ as your personal Savior. Recognize your deep need. You've sinned and it is separating you from God — breaking your heart and His. You must invite Him into your heart and life to live in you, to be on the throne of your life, and to guide and direct it. That is why He is trying to guide and advise us. He is not putting us down. He is not trying to keep us under His thumb. He is trying to say, "I made you. I created you. I know and understand everything about you, everything that's built into you, every weakness, strength and potential." He says, "Doesn't it make sense that I can help you, help you to understand better how to get the most out of yourself? How to experience all that I have for you?"

He loves us and He wants us to be happy. He doesn't want us to hurt. He wants us to able to cope with our problems and difficulties. He wants to set us free because He has a plan for our lives with a future and a hope, not. calamity! To receive His input, you must be born again. We can no more be a spiritual being without a spiritual birth, than we can be a physical being without a physical birth (John 3:5,6). We don't have to understand that, but we do have to accept it. I don't understand how a brown cow can eat grass and give white milk, but I still drink it. I see the miracle of a baby's birth and I don't understand that, but I can rejoice in it! There are so many things which I do not fully understand that I can still experience. The new birth is one of these. It is indispensable.

2. The second of the eight steps is that you must BE FILLED WITH THE SPIRIT. This is the command of Ephesians 5:18. It is not an option for the child of God. It's an imperative in the Greek language of the New Testament. He did not say, "If you feel like it, you ought to be filled." He says, "Be filled!" There is absolutely no way you can live a Christian life apart from the filling of the Holy Spirit. He is our energizer and dynamic. Literally, we are commanded to "be filled up full of God." That means turning control of our lives over to the Holy Spirit, and out of that control comes the ability to live the Christian life. In His power we see the really exciting and miraculous things happen.

*Chapter 7: Defeating Depresion*

There are four basic steps to being filled with the Spirit. They are the same steps involved in every spiritual decision or turning point. They are the same processes by which you come to know Christ as your personal Savior. You must recognize the NEED for Him to control your life. You must have a DESIRE for Him to take control. Third, you must CONFESS in repentance to God whatever sins He brings to mind. Don't become deeply introspective. There is no need for that. He won't dredge up all the garbage, but He will lovingly and gently show you some things, if you'll listen. He'll remind you, "Remember the anger and resentment you had," and you say, "Yes, Lord;" that's confession — just "agreeing with God." You're no longer copping out, and you're no longer unrepentant because you've come in line with God. You say, "God, that's right, that is the way I felt. I was wrong, I'm sorry, and I don't want it any more." It is that simple and basic.

As those walls come down through confession, His forgiveness comes through to us (I John 1:9,10). He forgave us on the cross, but that wall of anger and resentment prevents it from coming through on a practical level. Through Christ's atonement on the cross, we receive God's forgiveness for all our sins when we are born again. But this takes place in our spirit area. The soul area (mental, emotional) frequently is not set free until we confess certain specific sins and receive God's cleansing on an emotional level as well as on a spiritual level. (Remember, I John 1:9,10 was written to Christians, not unbelievers!). Only after we've done this in the area of our load-bearing hurts are we ready and able to forgive the person who's hurt us. Without the confession we do not receive specific forgiveness and thus have none to pass along to our offender. So we end up forgiving, but not forgetting. You cannot pass on what you do not possess and we receive forgiveness on the basis of our confession (Chapter 5 dealt with this concept in much more detail).

The fourth step in being filled with the Spirit is by faith to RECEIVE Him. It doesn't have to involve any emotional feeling at all. We are led astray over and over again by our feelings. They can be very fickle. So by faith you accept, "God wants me filled with his Spirit. I've asked Him to fill me,. Therefore it is done." That's as simple a logic as you can find. It is God's kind of logic.

## *Walk in the Spirit*

3. The third basic step in preventing depression is also vital. You must LEARN TO WALK IN THE SPIRIT (Galatians 5:25). This is more crucial in many ways than being filled with the Spirit. You can't walk if you aren't filled, but once you turn control over to the Holy Spirit, you must learn how to leave it there. I know of nothing so vital to this as what I call spiritual communion

time — the time you spend alone with God, basically in what we call Bible study and prayer. You cannot remain filled with the Spirit, nor walk in the spirit, if you don't spend time alone with the Father, getting to know Him and His love.

When we are born again, it is our spirit that is reborn. But there are two other parts to our being, soul and body, and they are not born again at that moment. In fact the Bible says, in the Old Testament, that the soul must be restored. (Psalm 23:3). The New Testament terminology is "renewing the mind" (Romans 12:2). The Old Testament word in the Hebrew for "restore" and the New Testament Word in the Greek for "renew" mean basically the same thing. They imply a major remodeling, or renovation. God says when our spirit has been born again that we must begin to work with Him in the remodeling of our soul or mind area. It includes our thoughts, will, emotions, memory and imagination. This takes some work to remodel, doesn't it? But this is where our problems are!

Satan never attacks us in our spirit — he attacks us in our soul! If we allow him to take lodging in our thoughts, it will show up on the screen of our imagination. If we let it take root there, we'll find it affecting our emotions and our will. It moves from there to our bodies. When it shows up in our body, it is already deeply rooted in our soul or mind area and is probably feeding on negative, hurting memories.

It is imperative that you learn to walk in the Spirit and begin immersing yourself in the Word of God so He can renew your mind. The world programs us 24 hours a day. If you spend ten minutes a day in God's Word, how can you expect to reverse the other 23 hours and 50 minutes? You can't do it! You must cut down the input in some of those other areas.

It is a matter of restructuring priorities. I can easily have a problem with the newspaper. If I'm not careful, I can spend 30-45 minutes a day reading it. On the other hand, when I don't read the paper for a few days, I find that I have missed very little significance. I still want to see the news more than anything else on TV, but if I miss the news for a week while on a trip, I find I can pick right back up. Things in the world don't really change all that much. I'm not saying that we should be ignorant about the world in which we live, only that we should not be dominated or controlled by it.

As we begin to restrict and control the world's input and increase God's, our perspective will begin to change. This will help Him to "brain wash" us, allowing Him to clean out our soul and mind area and renew it with His spiritual perspective on things. Instead of having the world's philosophy in us, we must have God's, because the mind is similar to a tremendously sophisticated computer. Computer programmers have a little saying in computer lingo called G-I-G-O — "garbage in, garbage out."

The only thing that comes out of a computer is what has been programmed into it. That is all that comes out of us. If it comes out of us, it is because it went into us. The problem is that so much of it goes into us when we're not even aware of it. I tell people to go to bed listening to teachings. They say, "But I always fall asleep." I say, "Great, it will keep right on going into your subconscious — just as commercials do. God's Word can do the same thing." It is better to listen consciously, but I'm saying, program yourself with the Word of God. Practice Philippians 4:8: "Whatsoever is pure, whatsoever is good, whatsoever is lovely, whatsoever is of good report, if there is any virtue, think on those things." As you do, God will begin to re-program your mind. It is vital to walk in the Spirit, to spend time in His Word and talking with and listening to Him. We must use each of the five basic aspects of prayer: praise, thanksgiving, confession, intercession, and petition, for each is vital to a dynamic relationship with God.

## *Count Your Blessings*

4. The fourth basic step in preventing depression is to THANK GOD IN ALL THINGS. I Thessalonians 5:18 says, "Rejoice in all things for this is the will of God in Christ Jesus concerning you." It doesn't mean that everything which happens to you is God's will; not at all! But what it does mean is you are to be thankful in every experience, and when you are, Romans 8:28 begins to come into play. You will begin to look for the good that God has in that experience. It doesn't have to be a good experience for Him to bring good out of it! You don't have to wallow in the bad experiences and settle for them. He is in the business of turning bad into good and bringing triumph out of tragedy. and He'll do it any time we allow Him.

Cultivate an attitude of gratitude. How do you do that? One way is to count your blessings! How long has it been since you thanked God for your eyelashes? You don't think they are important? They filter the dust and dirt out of your eyes. Cut them off and see. How long has it been since you thanked God for your earlobes? You don't think they do anything? Talk to someone who doesn't have any and find out how it affects their hearing. How long has it been since you thanked God for your thumb? Try picking up a pencil and writing without the use of your thumb. How long has it been since you thanked God for your big toe? Talk to someone who doesn't have a big toe and tries to walk barefoot and you'll find they have a difficult time even keeping their balance.

We have a million things we've never thought about for which to be thankful! We get so deep in self-pity that all we see are three or four bad things and we let them dominate and decimate our life and bring us to the point of depression. Start thanking God! Thank Him for your kneecaps. Thank Him for your blood vessels. Thank Him for your liver and your spleen — anything that works! Thank Him for it! Thank Him that your nose runs; some people's noses don't do anything! — so thank Him for it. Thank Him for the teeth you have that are yours. Thank Him for any false teeth that are paid for. Thank Him, thank Him, thank Him!

Cultivate an attitude of gratitude and I guarantee it will revolutionize your life! A Christian ought to be a grateful person because he, as no one else in all the world, ought to understand how much there is for which to be grateful. The sad fact is most Christians are not much more grateful overall than nonbelievers. We live like pagans and act like heathens and it breaks the heart of God. Count your blessings!

## *No Self-Pity*

5. Fifth, REJECT SELF-PITY. It is absolutely imperative. Anyone can feel sorry for himself and anyone who does is going to be hurt by it! Self-pity has never helped anyone with anything. One of the greatest blessings I had as a pastor was visiting the hospitals. Not because I enjoyed it, but because it helped to keep things in perspective. It kept me from feeling sorry for myself when others had it so much worse. There used to be a sign on the wall of the parking lot at one of Tulsa's hospitals. It said, "I cried because I had no shoes, until I met a man who had no feet." I went to college with people who had no feet, who had no hands. I remember walking into a large room one day at the university and hearing the most beautiful music coming from the piano. I walked over to listen to the young lady playing. Looking down I saw that she did not have one complete finger on either of her hands. She had learned to rejoice in the Lord, to use what she had. She had no time for self-pity. She was one of the most radiant, joyful people I ever met.

## *We're at War!*

6. The sixth basic step to overcoming depression is to UNDERSTAND SPIRITUAL WARFARE. I guarantee you it is real and very few Christians really understand this fact. What do you think would happen to a nation that was at war and didn't know it? They would soon be defeated, wouldn't they? This is exactly the way most Christians are. It is guerilla warfare. The devil has been defeated but he is still skirmishing all the time. The best illustration

*Chapter 7: Defeating Depresion*

I know of today on the human scene was Russia moving in and taking over Afghanistan in 1980. They won the war, but some of the Afghans don't know that. They are still fighting guerilla warfare and killing Russians every day. Now that's the kind of warfare in which we are engaged. It is talked about in Ephesians 6:10-13 (NASB): "Finally be strong in the Lord and in the strength of His might. Put on the full armor of God, that you may be able to stand firm against the schemes of the devil. For our struggle is not against flesh and blood, but against the rulers, against the powers, against the world force of this darkness, against the spiritual forces of wickedness in the heavenly places. Therefore take up the full armor of God that you may be able to resist in the evil day, and having done everything, to stand firm."

We are either at war or God is a liar, and He doesn't lie! We are at war and we need to realize it. We must come to understand our enemy and how he fights. The Bible says we are not to be ignorant of his strategy and the way he works. One of the reasons psychiatry and psychology are relatively fruitless in many areas of counseling is because they do not understand spiritual warfare. They do not even allow for it. Most of them do not allow the power of God to work through them. I'm talking in general, not of every psychiatrist and psychologist. Many of these men I can't blame because they do not know, but a child of God ought to know! II Corinthians 10, verses 3, 4, and 5 say, "For though we walk in the flesh, we not war according to the flesh" (He says that we are at war, but it is not human warfare). "For the weapons of our warfare are not of the flesh or human ones, but divinely powerful to do four things: for pulling down strongholds; for casting down imaginations; every high thing raised up against the knowledge of God; and for taking every thought captive in obedience to Christ." He has given us power to do that and Christians must master each of the four. We need understanding in each area if we are going to be successful in the Christian life.

Understand spiritual warfare. It is real. God's power is required, and our cooperation with God is essential. James 4:7 tells us how to cooperate with God. When most people quote that verse, though, they omit the first part of the verse. "Submit yourselves therefore to the Lord and resist the devil and he will flee." Try to resist the devil on your own and he will run you down! It isn't enough just to resist him. You must also be submissive to the Lord, as the first of the verse admonishes us. Satan has no power and authority over you as a child of God, but you must understand your spiritual authority and exercise it. When you know that and resist him, he will have to flee. If you flee, he will eat you up!

## *The Armor of God*

In Ephesians 6:14-18 we read of the armor of God. One of the interesting things as we study this armor is to find that it covers only the front and the sides. There is none for the back side. So when we cut and run, we're defenseless. God doesn't want us to be cowards. He wants us to stand strong in His strength and in the power of His might and when we do, the devil will flee. So it is imperative that we understand spiritual warfare, which is a whole different study in itself (see teaching entitled, *Our Position in Christ* for help in this area).

## *The 3 R's*

7. The seventh step to preventing depression is the three R's: REJECT, REBUKE, AND RECITE. Let me explain these for you. First, recognize and reject the wrong thoughts that come against you, because that is where Satan hits you. He tempts you with the wrong thought. The thought may be to feel sorry for yourself or to think, "I wonder what they meant by that?" Have you ever had that kind of thought? Well, it's a wrong thought. The next time it comes to mind, you will know who sent it. When he knocks at your door, refuse it — reject that thought. You must learn to take control of your thoughts (II Cor. 10:5). Martin Luther said hundreds of years ago, "You can't keep the birds from flying over your head, but you can keep them from building a nest in your hair!" Reject that thought which is wrong (self-defeating, counter-productive) for you. Wrong thoughts include fear, guilt, self-pity, lying, bitterness, worry, inferiority, self-righteousness, and despondency, to only name a few. Learn to recognize your particular wrong thoughts.

Second, rebuke the adversary. Take authority over the devil just as Jesus and the apostles did. Just as I must, so must you. Identify the enemy and command him to leave you alone in the name of Jesus. You have the authority as does every born again believer; it is part of our inheritance in Christ. Find out who the Bible says you are in Christ and come to know your authority in Him (see teachings 122 and 123).

Third, recite. Recite what God's Word says on the subject. Quit listening to what everybody else says on the matter. Listen to God — if the wisest person in the world lived next door to you and was always available to discuss any problem, wouldn't you take advantage of his wisdom? Well, He is. He is not only always available, but He has put it down in writing for us. He has made a totally dependable, written commitment to us. He always keeps His promises. Meet His conditions. Stand on them and claim them for your situation. He will make them alive to you and for you (see Appendix A for more help).

8. The eighth and final step in preventing depression is practicing the THREE STEPS TO INNER HEALING that I have discussed with you earlier (especially the first two): confess your wrong reactions, forgive the person who has hurt you, and forget the hurting experience. The third one you do through what we call prayer visioning, where God allows us to see what Jesus is doing to take all remaining sting and hurt out of that negative memory and experience (refer back to Chapter 2).

Let's review briefly what has been covered previously. The first step is to confess your wrong reactions. When you confess your wrong reactions, you are acknowledging your negative feelings towards yourself or another. It doesn't matter whether they are justifiable or not. They are wrong because they are bad for you. They are self-defeating. God loves you, and He doesn't want you to hurt. Understand that when we are hurt by others, we tend to have certain negative reactions, such as anger, resentment, bitterness, rebellion or fear. We need to become sensitive to this fact. Begin to get tough with yourself in recognizing these and purging them from your life. Don't let them stay and punish you further for what someone else has done to you.

## *Avoid Self-Punishment*

So many of the load-bearing hurts in people are at just this point. Unwittingly, we are punishing ourselves for what someone else did to us. Many times it is something that happened years ago. When we finally get around to dealing with it spiritually, we think in terms only of forgiveness — of them. We must do this; it looses God's forgiveness to us and I John 1:9 says that His forgiveness is like a disinfectant that "cleanses" us. This then releases us to be able to forgive them and ourselves, when necessary. Then our forgiving them for what they did to us allows God to stitch up the wound so that it can completely heal. To forgive without confessing is like stitching up an infected wound! It is bound to cause trouble again. This is why many times we can forgive and yet not forget! Remember, confession and forgiveness must become as Siamese twins — inseparable, if you want to be set free from your load-bearing hurts (re-study "The Story of Billy" in Chapter 2). You deserve to be set free from that hurt someone else brought to your life. The only way you are going to be set free is to confess your wrong reactions and forgive those who've hurt you. It is done by an act of your will and a step of faith. God loves you. He doesn't want you to hurt. Jesus always forgave this way.

Don't go on hurting for what somebody else did to you and don't get hung up on whether they deserve to be forgiven or not. It doesn't matter whether they deserve it or not; none of us deserves God's forgiveness, but He gives it! If God waited to forgive us until we deserved it, we never would have been forgiven, would we? One of the reasons that God so freely forgives us is because He knows until He gets us cleaned up, He can't use us to bless others. He not only loves us, He loves all the people who need our help. God taught me years ago that every blessing from Him comes to us on its way to somebody else. We are like the runner in a relay race, we just pass it on. Oh, that's where life is lived with a capital L! When we pass it on, God multiplies it and multiplies it!

Let me say one final thing very quickly about forgiveness. We not only have to forgive the person who hurt us, sometimes there is a sense in which we need to forgive God. Now people say to me, "How does one forgive God?" We don't really forgive Him for anything He's done. We simply use the process of forgiveness (release) to "forgive" God for what we felt He did, or didn't do. It is not for God's benefit; it is for ours. It simply helps us to realize that God never did what we thought He did. He never felt about us the way we thought. He felt. He was not uncaring and unconcerned. It just seemed that way. So we need to release those negative feelings toward Him. It is imperative to both our spiritual and emotional health.

Depression is both healable and preventable. Know it. Believe it. Expect it. You can come to the point of living a depression-free life, even when you have been bound by it for years! I am a living example of that fact and so can you be!

*Chapter 8*

# HOW TO DO INNER HEALING WITH YOURSELF

This is pre-eminently a self-help chapter. We are going to set forth a step-by-step process to help you do inner healing with yourself. It may be impossible or unnecessary for you to see a counselor. God can still heal you of those hurting memories just as He has me and countless others. I basically had no one to help me through this process except the Lord and as He has healed me, so He will you, if you are willing to pay the price involved. The guidelines contained in this chapter will make it easier.

III John 2 says, "Beloved I pray that in all respects you may prosper and be in good health just as your soul prospers." The Lord is a God of good health. He wants us healed and whole and is not the author of disease. He wants us to be healthy in every area of life: spiritually, emotionally, and physically. This verse also tells us that all prosperity in our lives is directly related to the health and vitality of our soul. Our soul, remember, is the mind area which encompasses five aspects: the thought processes, the will, the memory, the imagination, and the emotions. So what God is saying here is that if we really want to prosper and be in all around good health, we must prosper in our soul area. This speaks directly to the matter of inner healing. To the degree that we are healthy and balanced in our soul or mind area, we will be able to prosper more spiritually, emotionally, physically, financially and every other way.

Another exciting passage of scripture on this subject is found in Proverbs 3:1-8. Verses 1 and 2 state, 'My son, do not forget my teaching but let your heart keep my commandment, for length of days and years of life and peace they will add to you." Keeping the commandments of God will increase both the quantity and quality of the days of our lives. It will add a deep dimension of inner peace. In verses 3-8 He continues, "Do not let mercy and truth leave you. Bind them around your neck, write them on the tablet of your heart and you will find favor and good repute in the sight of both God and man. Trust in the Lord with all your heart and do not lean on your own understanding. In all your ways acknowledge Him and He will make your paths straight. Do not be wise in your own eyes. Fear the Lord and turn away from evil and it will be healing to your body and refreshment to your bones." Literally, it says, "It will be health to your body and refreshment to your bones."

Adherence to the principles of God's Word will help bring healing and refreshment to our body and being. We must live in His Word until it lives in us — becomes a dynamic force in our daily life. As we delight in the Lord (Psalm 37:4), He will be able more and more to give us the desires of our hearts because we'll find His desires becoming our desires. This is the pathway to healing and wholeness, the meeting of all our needs.

Remember that very moving passage of scripture in Psalm 142:7: "Bring my soul out of prison so that I may give thanks to thy name." If you have trouble praising God and rejoicing in the Lord, it may be because your soul is in prison. All prisons are not made of metal bars. Our soul can be imprisoned by the hurts in our lives. That's why the Bible teaches that our soul (mind) must be restored (renewed), or remodeled.

Don't become discouraged and give up when you feel the remodeling work is not progressing as rapidly as it should. Every remodeling job in which I've ever been involved moved more slowly than originally anticipated. Why? Because we run into things which we hadn't anticipated. It will probably be that way in your own inner healing process, but God will bring you through it with an even deeper healing. Remodeling just takes a little while.

## PART OF OUR HERITAGE

Now let's begin to review some guidelines for our healing. First, we must understand that healing is part of our heritage in Christ. God has provided it for our spirit, soul, and body. We need to be whole in all three areas. Healing of the spirit is salvation. It begins with the new birth and continues through a daily walk in the Spirit. Healing of the body can come in numerous ways. It comes first and primarily through the proper care of our bodies that God has given us. Secondly, when we do have problems, it comes through the use of doctors and nurses who are trained, skilled and gifted by God in this area. Third, it is essential that we understand that God is the Great Physician. Many years passed before I realized that it was as important for me to know God in this relationship as it was to know Him as Creator, Redeemer, and Lord. He is our Great Physician. He's the greatest diagnostician of all time and His prognosis is always correct. It is His desire for us to be whole and He will teach us how to stand on His Word in faith for healing. He will also allow us at times to receive the gift of healing through one of His anointed servants, as well as using us to pray for it in others. The Bible says when we lay hands on one another and pray for one another it will facilitate our healing (James 5:14-16). God has all of these ways through which He has made healing available to our bodies. Inner or emotional healing is another one of His provisions. It, too, is part of our Christian heritage.

## INNER HEALING

God has numerous ways of doing inner healing. Some have so equated prayer visioning with inner healing that many people think it is the only way God does it. This is not so. God has never been limited in doing healing by one method, whether it's physical or emotional. He has many ways.

Let me briefly share with you some of the ways God does inner healing. When we are born again, inner healing takes place as well as when we are filled with the Spirit. As we walk under the Spirit's control, it continues though we may not even be aware of it — it may not be dramatic, flashy or emotional, but it's still going on, because that is part of God's promise to us. As we continue to confess our sin and forgive others, inner healing is taking place.

Self-discipline promotes healing as does openness and honesty about ourselves and others. Ministering to the needs of others allows God to minister to us, so as we minister to others and help them in the name of Jesus, we will be assisting our own inner healing. Standing on the promises of God's Word renews our mind and facilitates healing. The ministry of the Holy Spirit in our lives, even while we're asleep, continues our healing. Learning to thank God in all things, praising Him in every situation, pulling down strongholds, rebuking spirits, praying in tongues are just some of the ways through which He can minister healing to us. Knowing our position in Christ is one of the greatest methods of inner healing that I know of, as we come to realize what it means to be a joint heir with Jesus.

## HEALING OF MEMORIES

The heart of all inner healing is the healing of our hurting memories. They are the ones which cause our hang-ups and in turn produce childish attitudes and actions on our part. The healing of the hurting, negative memories is absolutely imperative to real emotional health, regardless of which method is used by God. Memories can either motivate or devastate us. As God heals the detrimental aspects of our memories, we are released to function in line with our full potential and can really begin to experience the abundant life about which Jesus taught.

Since this healing and wholeness are so crucial to the quality of one's Christian life, it is important that we understand the principles of this chapter clearly and precisely. IT IS MY DESIRE THAT YOU BE ABLE TO DO THIS HEALING WITH YOURSELF, as much as possible. That's the ultimate purpose of this book.

You may never be able to see a counselor, but you do not have to continue carrying all of your hurts. Go to an inner healing counselor, if and when you can, but don't be totally dependent on one. LEARN TO TRUST GOD DIRECTLY, and see what He will do.

The hub of the process is outlined in detail in Chapter Two, and it revolves around those three simple, but intricate steps. Let's review them again one final time.

## CONFESS WRONG REACTIONS

First, confess your wrong reactions towards those who have hurt you. Confess those feelings and attitudes of anger, resentment, rebellion and fear. You must become deeply convinced that they are wrong for you. Wrong, not because they are necessarily unjustified, but basically because they are bad for you. Bad, because they are self-defeating and counter-productive — they distort your perspective. Wrong, because they hurt you and ones you love. God loves us and doesn't want us to hurt ourselves or others. Not only do they not bring one positive benefit to your life, they are extremely self-destructive. We hurt both ourselves and loved ones by hanging on to these negative memories.

The irony of ironies is that we allow the people who have hurt us the most to continue pulling our emotional strings by retaining negative attitudes towards them. In our ignorance and obstinacy, we are indeed practicing self-punishment! We are unwittingly punishing ourselves for what someone else has done to us, and they go on hurting us year after year. That's not dumb, it's stupid! (I can't help being dumb or uninformed about some things, but I don't want to be stupid, do you?)

How tragic that the people whom I often want to affect me least could actually affect me most and then cause me, by the hurts they inflicted on me, to react the most to those whom I love best. That vicious cycle can and must be broken in our lives. We can be set free in Christ. For when we know the truth, the knowing of it can liberate us from this devastating cycle (John 8:32).

Much of the key is found in this matter of confession. To "confess" means to "agree with God" that what He is saying to us is right (and He always is right whether we understand it or not). He wants to show us not only where we hurt, but why we hurt. He wants us to see that negative attitudes are wrong because they are self-defeating. You see, sin is not sin in the emotional sense because we violate rule #93 on God's list of no-no's. Sin is sin in the emotional sense because it is a wrong reaction for us. Wrong because it's bad for us and short-circuits what God wants to do in us to conform us to the image of Christ. A reaction because we've allowed negative feelings to layer up until they've created a negative attitude. FEELINGS ARE NOT NECESSARILY WRONG, BUT ATTITUDES ARE. Feelings (or responses) simply must be recognized and properly dealt with to prevent them from growing in a negative manner. Attitudes (or reactions) are a different matter. They are what produce "strongholds" (II Corinthians 10:3-4) in our lives which give open access to our adversary, the devil.

## *Wait Before Him*

We must confess or agree with God about them. As we are willing to pay the price of waiting before Him, He will show us what we need to confess. Then we must acknowledge, "God you're right. I see now that that is how I've felt. It's wrong and I'm sorry. I release it to You in confession."

This allows God, then, to take it away from us once and for all. It also does two other crucial things: it releases God's forgiveness into us (so we can pass it along) and it brings His cleansing of that emotional wound. God's forgiveness coming from our confession acts as a cleansing agent (like peroxide or iodine) which washes out the emotional infection in the hurting memory. This sterilization of the emotional wound is essential to deep inner healing. Only after we have done this are we really ready to take step two in the healing process.

## FORGIVE ... FORGIVE

Second, we must forgive those who have hurt us. Not to forgive would again be self-defeating. Because we have been forgiven through our confession, we are not able to forgive. We can only pass on what we possess, and we receive forgiveness through our act of confession. (As I've stated in an earlier chapter, real New Testament confession always involves repentance, because we have changed our mind and come in line with what God says on the matter.)

Now we must do what we are able to do — forgive. It is a lie from the pit of hell to believe that we are not able to forgive someone. Yes, we can! We can forgive anyone we need to by an act of our will and a child-like step of faith. Following the three steps of inner healing as I'm outlining not only allows us to forgive but also to forget.

## 3 Stumbling Blocks

Remember as I said in "The Story of Billy" in Chapter 2, there are three main excuses that tend to trip us up: "I don't feel like it," "They don't deserve it," and "I want to get back at them." Failing to forgive for these reasons will hurt us far more than it will hurt those by whom we've been hurt. It will allow a wall of unforgiveness to develop in us which will cut us off from God's healing love. Even an all-powerful, loving God cannot penetrate our willful unforgiveness.

## Own Worst Enemy

It's important for us to "get smart" at this point. We are our own worst enemy. We punish ourselves all the time by not understanding and/or not cooperating with God's principles. They are designed only to help, not hurt us. Begin to SEE CONFESSION AND FORGIVENESS AS SIAMESE TWINS, and practice them "religiously". Go back to Chapter 2 and read and re-read "The Story of Billy" until the principles illustrated by it are part of your very being. This will cost you in time, energy, and prayer, but it will be worth it. It will result in your progressive healing and wholeness.

Realize that it is particularly crucial to the process of healing that we confess and forgive in relation to the load-bearing hurts. As I stated in Chapter 5 on forgiveness, these key hurts are of two types: those where SOMEONE ELSE HAS HURT YOU and those where YOU HAVE HURT ANOTHER. (Obviously, most hurts are a combination of these two.)

## Don't Take Shortcuts

When others have hurt us and we come around to dealing with it spiritually, we tend to try to forgive without thinking about confessing. Doing this gives us some emotional release, but we have, in effect, tried to stitch up an infected wound and we cannot gain lasting relief. We are unable to forget the hurt, because we haven't released it through confession.

In those instances where we recognize that we have hurt someone else, the problem usually is just the reverse. We tend to confess our sin, or wrong reaction, but not to forgive. Thus, we are sterilizing the emotional wound without stitching (forgiveness) it closed. While this helps temporarily, it cannot go long until it is reinfected. We do not forgive because our mind says, "Who is there to forgive? I did it." Of course the answer is that we must forgive ourselves. This is the other area where the healing process so often breaks down in Christians. We are not usually good at forgiving ourselves. Our mind says, "I can't do it. It's not that simple," but it is. We forgive ourselves just as we do anyone else, as an act of our will and a simple step of faith. Then we reject the accusations of our feelings. Feelings have nothing to do with biblical forgiveness. We must remember that and reject them.

## PRAYER VISIONING

Now let's focus briefly on the third step of the inner healing process — prayer visioning. Perhaps it is the most miraculous aspect of the healing sequence and is frequently misunderstood. As I have stated earlier, it is simply not psychological visualization (which takes place in the soul area), but rather it is an experience which God gives us in prayer which is discerned by our spirit. In its essence it is simply God showing us in prayer what Jesus is doing to meet the existing need in our life — healing that hurting memory which has limited our response-ability to the Father.

There is no way to intellectually understand prayer visioning. It simply is to be experienced spiritually and received emotionally. Under God's anointing it heals the deepest kinds of hurts — rape, incest, child molestation and abuse, death, divorce, and on and on. It takes place only one time with any given hurt, and it heals forever, removing the emotional scar tissue. It takes away the hurt, pain, and sting of the traumatic memory. And the acid test — it works!

Any Christian can have this healing encounter with God. You can experience it with yourself in the Lord — believers all over the world have. It's God's gift to you in sealing the healing of that hurting memory. It is of inestimable value when applied at the point of a specific load-bearing hurt.

Specific, pointed and practical — that's what both you and I want this chapter to be, so let's sharpen our focus even more. Here is a step-by-step process for you to follow.

1. CREATE A CLIMATE CONDUCIVE TO HEALING. Have a time daily to be alone with God, preferably at the beginning of the day. Spend time in the Word and prayer in communion with your heavenly Father. Get to know Him and to love Him and bask in His love of you.

2. GET INTO THE FLOW OF HIS SPIRIT. Confess your desire to be both submissive and sensitive to Him. Learn to wait quietly before Him in a spirit of meditation. Listening, rather than talking. (This is probably the best time to use regularly for inner healing also. Try to expand your devotional time to include a few moments daily waiting before the Lord to show you any memories to be healed.)

3. REBUKE ANY SPIRITS WHICH SEEM TO COME AGAINST YOU. Be sure that they will try to prevent this time and process. Remember that you are in spiritual warfare (II Corinthians 10:3-4). Know that you fight against spiritual beings, but with spiritual weapons (Ephesians 6:10-18). God would not have you to be ignorant about this (II Corinthians 2:11).

4. IDENTIFY THE SPIRITS BY YOUR NEGATIVE EMOTIONS and the distractions you encounter — spirits such as indifference, distraction, confusion, hindrance, restlessness, self-deception, and spiritual blindness. Cease the foolish thinking that these are simply mental problems. They are that, but more, or God's Word is not correct.

5. EXPECTANTLY ASK GOD TO BRING TO YOUR MIND MEMORIES WHICH NEED HEALING. Do not work at it through deep introspection of self-analysis. Wait before Him in praise and thanksgiving, confession and forgiveness. If nothing seems to materialize after spending some time waiting, then you might. . .

6. TAKE A BACKWARD WALK THROUGH YOUR MEMORIES. Start with your senior year in high school or when you were eighteen years old. Take one grade or year at a time, reflecting upon it to see if God wants to surface any memories from that period. Then move to the previous grade or year until you have walked back to when you began school. Next do the same thing with the preschool years. Examine any hurting memory which surfaces and go through the three steps to inner healing. You can also start at eighteen (or any year) and move forward. Remember, the key is not how much you recall, but that you do it in expectant faith, creating a conducive climate and allowing yourself to hear what God is saying. He wants to help and heal you.

7. DEAL WITH EACH SIGNIFICANT HURT INDIVIDUALLY. Ask the Holy Spirit to help you discern HOW YOU FELT AT THE TIME. What were your negative reactions then that have grown? Don't assume they have somehow "disappeared" if the original hurt was significant. Then confess those reactions and forgive that person and/or yourself. (Don't overlook your feelings towards God and the need to confess them! Everyone gets mad at God at times.)

8. WAIT BEFORE THE LORD WITH EYES CLOSED (to avoid distractions), ASKING HIM TO LET YOU SEE (or sense) WHAT JESUS IS DOING to complete the inner healing process through prayer visioning. DON'T TRY TO IMAGINE ANYTHING. As much as you

*Chapter 8: How to Do Inner Healing with Yourself*

can, put your intellect on "hold" or "automatic pilot." Prayer visioning must be experienced in your spirit for the deepest level of healing. Be patient and expectant on a daily basis. Give God time. Don't be discouraged if nothing seems to happen when you first try. Be persistent in going before Him, showing that you really desire to be set free. Realize, also, that YOU DON'T HAVE TO "SEE" ANYTHING as we think of seeing. We are not dealing with either the physical or mind's eyes. IT IS SEEING OR SENSING IN YOUR SPIRIT. When this occurs, there will be a sense of God's peace and presence which comes.

9. DO NOT BECOME ANXIOUS if a memory surfaces and you cannot gain peace about it at the time. Try again later. GIVE GOD TIME to undo what has taken years to build. The hurt may still be too great for you to deal with at this point. Place it on the "back burner" and allow it to simmer for awhile. Memory healing is like peeling the layers of an onion. It will come step by step, layer by layer.

10. KEEP A LIST OF THE HURTING MEMORIES WHICH GOD BRINGS BACK AND WHAT YOU DID WITH EACH of them, as far as the three healing steps, confession, forgiveness, and prayer visioning, are concerned. Otherwise, you will tend to be deceived over a period of time, believing you have done healing with a memory simply because you remember God bringing it to mind. This isn't necessary if you don't really hurt much and aren't having any real reactions, but it certainly is if you do and seriously want to be set free as quickly and completely as possible. DON'T PLAY GAMES LIKE SO MANY DO. Denying or repressing the memory is not forgetting it, just as recognizing and dealing with it is not negative confession. Be honest with God and yourself, or you won't be healed. Realize, though, that while "honesty is the best policy", it is also painful to come degree. It is a growing pain — the pain of healing.

11. LEARN TO LISTEN TO WHAT YOUR EMOTIONS ARE SAYING, just as you are training yourself to hear God more clearly. I'll guarantee both of them are speaking to you far more than you have ever realized. Your hurting emotions speak to you through tension, anxiety, guilt, fear, impatience, headaches, stomach pains and a myriad of additional ways. Ask God to show you why you hurt where you do and why things affect you the way they do. Come to understand the logic of your emotions and the process through which you go in moving from a response to a reaction level as set forth in The Inner Healing Reactions Chart. First, we experience sufficient rejection

in a given area to develop a sense of rejection, which in turn, produces a fear of rejection that generates a sense of self-rejection, leading to a problem of low self-image in that area. As this sequence is repeated, the basic emotions of anger and fear begin to move to the reaction level in that area of our emotions because we have more hurting memories in that area than we can easily manage. (Review Chapter 2).

12. UNDERSTAND THE DIFFERENCE BETWEEN A RESPONSE AND A REACTION. Check the glossary for my basic definition and work it down deep into your being until you easily recognize the difference in yourself and in your significant others. Let your areas of reaction become as searchlights to illuminate where you hurt and why you are reacting. Concentrate on being released from your wrong reactions and not on what others have done to you (or you will always be the loser in those experiences). Desire healing and wholeness for your own sake, not for someone else's. At some point you must begin to care enough about yourself to commit to doing what's really best for you. Begin to see and love yourself as God does — you are worth it!

13. FINALLY, ACCEPT THE FACT THERE IS NO HEALING WITHOUT PAIN, BUT... it is nothing like you fear. Nor is it anything like the pain of going on in bondage to your hurts and fears. Healing only hurts for a little while, as God resurfaces those memories for one last time to heal you and set you free forever. Believe with all your heart that He wants to give you "Healing Where You Hurt... On The Inside."

# INNER HEALING GLOSSARY*

1. COMPLEX. Something is thought of as complex when it seems so complicated that it appears confusing and overwhelming to us. Man has a tendency towards complexity.

2. CONFESS. Literally means "to agree with God" that what He is saying to you is right. This involves both the negative confession of sin and/or wrong reactions, as well as the positive confession of and agreement with God's Word in any given area.

3. FORGIVE. Tb release all negative attitudes towards another for our sake as well as theirs. We do not have to feel like it emotionally to do so. Do it because it is right to do so. It is an act of our will and a step of faith on our part, just as it was with Jesus.

4. INTRICATE. One large whole made up of many individual but interrelated parts. What God does is intricate, but not complex.

5. LOAD-BEARING HURTS. These are the most significant emotional hurts in one's life. They are the ones which much be discerned and healed for the internal stress to be released.

6. PARTITION HURTS. These are the less significant emotional hurts in our lives. It is not usually crucial for these to be healed in the inner healing process.

7. REACTION. A reaction is the opposite of a response. We are more upset than the situation justifies and we have much more difficulty dealing with it. Usually we end up repressing or burying our feeling.

8. REJECTION. Any experience where one perceives that he did not receive the love, acceptance, affirmation or approval which he needs in the way he needs it, when he needs it, and from whom he needs it. It may be either real or imagined and is usually a combination of the two. It is the root of all emotional hurt related to people.

9. RESPONSE. To respond to an irritating situation means two things. We are not more upset than the situation warrants and we are able to deal with that upset in a proper manner.

10. SOUL. One of three areas of man's being, along with our spirit and body. Basically, it is the mind area and is composed of five aspects: thoughts, will, memory, imagination, and emotions.

*These are the author's definitions of the above words and terms. They do not necessarily agree with the meaning which others give to them.

*Appendix A*

# VICTORY IN YOUR THOUGHT-LIFE

The Bible says that we are at W-A-R, and the sad matter of fact is that many Christians do not even really know it. At least they are unaware that it is not a human warfare. God's Word tells us that we fight against "the rulers. . . powers . . . world forces of darkness . . . spiritual forces of wickedness in heavenly places." (Eph. 6:12). Paul urges us to "be strong in the Lord and in the strength of His might," (Eph. 6:10) and to "take every thought captive in obedience to Christ," (II Cor. 10:5).

One will live a defeated spiritual life until they begin to take these verses seriously. We are at war, and THE BATTLE IS FOR THE MIND. This is where the adversary and his army of spirits attack believers. The assault is continuous and we must learn how to do battle. The Bible says we must "not (be) ignorant of his strategies" (II Cor. 2:11).

We must begin to learn how to have victory in our thought-lives. To this end let me share 5 R's that have been helpful to me and hundreds of others I've taught.

1. RECOGNIZE AND REJECT THE WRONG THOUGHTS (negative or tempting) which come against you (II Cor. 10:5). We must understand that any thought that is BAD for us is a wrong thought. Thus, it is wrong or bad to think any thought which is Self-Defeating or Counter-Productive. Christians Must Become Tough-Minded. Begin to realize that thoughts like Self-Pity, Resentment, Fear, Guilt, Negativism, Jealousy, Worry, and Discouragement are wrong thoughts! They are BAD for you and self-defeating. So recognize this as a fact and reject them. Don't accept them in your mind.

2. REBUKE THE APPROPRIATE SPIRIT IN THE STRONG NAME OF JESUS. Evil spirits are real. They are simply Satan's army for use against his enemy — the people of God. You can usually identify which ones are harassing you by the negative emotions which are present (e.g. anxiety, depression, hatred, rage, rebellion, loneliness, sadness, fantasy, unbelief, etc.). They feed on our negative emotions and hurts, infecting and worsening them. But the Bible tells us that we have authority over them in

Christ. (Matt. 16:19, II Cor. 10:4-5, Mark 16:17, James 4:7). We can and must command them to leave us alone.

3. RECITE WHAT GOD'S WORD SAYS about your problem area, and RENEW YOUR MIND in it. (Romans 12:2). We are indoctrinated continuously by the world's point of view. (That's why the viewpoint of so many Christians is basically the same as non-Christians!). If you want to see victory in your life, YOU MUST BEGIN TO VIEW LIFE FROM GOD'S PERSPECTIVE instead of the world's. This involves learning to stand against circumstances and so stand on God's Word. You must live in the Word until it comes alive in you and dominates and controls your thinking. Look up these scriptures (if you're not already familiar with them) and begin to let them permeate you and transform your thinking. (I Cor. 10:13; Psalm 138:8; Phil. 4:4,13,19; II Tim. 1:17; I Thess. 5:18; Romans 8:28; Gal. 5:22-5; II Cor. 10:3-5).

4. RESIST THE DEVIL and he will flee from you! (James 4:7) God didn't make us to be runners. He wants us to be resistors! He wants us to put on His full armor (Eph. 6:11-17), stop running, and start fighting. (There is no armor for our backside!) When we do, we will be victorious over him!

5. REJOICE IN ALL THINGS for this is the will of God concerning you. (I Thess. 5:18) It is essential that Christians continuously cultivate an attitude of gratitude. We must be a grateful people, giving thanks in all things. This passage is not saying that everything which happens to us is what God desires for us. What He is saying is that we are to learn to rejoice and be thankful in all things, because this kind of attitude is His will for us. It is not enough to merely "give thanks" when we feel like it or when the circumstance is to our liking. The real discipline and blessing of this teaching come in being obedient. Such obedience will lift burdens, change your perspective, and bless you in countless ways. If you will incorporate these five principles into your life and internalize them into your spirit, you will find increasing victory in your thought-life. Then you will come to experience more and more the promise of Jesus in John 10:10 concerning a really abundant life! "I came that (you) might have life and might have it abundantly."

*Appendix B*

# HOW TO BE BORN AGAIN—SPIRITUALLY

The most important topic which you will ever consider concerns your relationship with almighty God. It is one which requires a personal decision from each of us — whether we will accept or reject His only son, Jesus Christ.

The Bible, God's Holy Word, explains how anyone may actually come to have a personal relationship with Jesus through an experience of spiritual rebirth. It requires recognizing and receiving the following facts as truth from God.

I) GOD LOVES YOU AND WANTS YOU TO KNOW HIM!

    A) His love is total... John 3:16
"For God so loved the world, that He gave His only Son, that whoever believes in Him should not perish, but have eternal life."

    B) He wants us to know Him
All other religions of the world are the story of men seeking after God, but Christianity is the story of God seeking man, and sending His only Son to find them.
"This is love: not that we loved God, But that He loved us and sent His Son an atoning sacrifice for our sins." (I John 4:10, NIV)

II) OUR SIN SEPARATES US FROM GOD'S LOVE

    A) Every person has sinned
"There is none righteous, not even one." (Romans 3:10)
"If we say that we have no sin, we are deceiving ourselves, and the truth is not in us." (1 John 1:8)

    B) Our sin separates us from Him
"For all have sinned and fallen short of the glory of God." (Romans 3:23)
"For the wages of sin is death . . ."

III) GOD IN HIS LOVE HAS PAID IN FULL THE PENALTY FOR OUR SIN

    A) Jesus paid it all

"But God demonstrates His own love toward us, in that while we were yet sinners, Christ died for us" (Romans 5:8)

"... the free gift of God is eternal life in Christ Jesus our Lord." (Romans 6:23b)

"See how great a love the Father has bestowed upon us, that we should be called the children of God ..." (I John 3:1)

IV) WE MUST EACH RECEIVE HIM INTO OUR LIVES PERSONALLY TO BE SAVED

    A) Receiving Jesus as Savior makes us God's children
"... as many as received Him, to them He gave the right to become the children of God, even to those who believe in His name." (John 1:12)

    B) Our confession brings his forgiveness
"If we confess our sins, He is faithful and righteous to forgive us our sins and to cleanse us from all unrighteousness." (I John 1:9)

V) WE RECEIVE HIS SAVING LOVE BY FAITH

    A) "For by grace you have been saved through faith and that not of yourselves, it is the gift of God: not as a result of (good) works, that no one should boast." (Ephesians 2:8,9)

VI) WE MUST CONFESS HIM AND BELIEVE IN HIM

    A) "... if you confess with your mouth (that) Jesus is Lord, and believe in your heart that God raised Him from the dead, you shall be saved; for with the heart man believes, resulting in righteousness, and with the mouth he confesses, resulting in salvation." (Romans 10:9,10)

VII) RECEIVE HIM NOW BY PRAYING THIS SIMPLE PRAYER

    A) "Dear Jesus, I recognize my need for you, confess my sins to you, and receive you into my heart and life by faith now. I thank you for forgiving and cleansing me and for taking up residence in my life to guide me and direct me in my daily living. Thank you for making me your child and a joint-heir with Jesus Christ."

VIII) HAVE THE ASSURANCE THAT HE HAS DONE WHAT YOU ASKED HIM TO DO

    A) The Bible was written to help give you this confidence.
"These things have I written to you who believe in the name of the

Son of God, in order that you may know that you have eternal life. And this is the confidence which we have before Him, that, if we ask anything according to His will, He hears us. And if we know that He hears us in whatever we ask, we know that we have the requests which we have asked form Him." (I John 5:13-15)

B) Our feelings make no difference
Our faith is in Jesus and the fact of His Word, not in our emotional feelings which are fickle and undependable.

IX) NOW WALK WITH HIM AND LIVE FOR HIM

A) Spend time in daily prayer communion (Luke 11:9,10; Phil. 4:6-8; Col. 4:2)

B) Read the Bible regularly (Acts 17:11; Prov. 4:20-22; Joshua 1:8; Psalm 119:11,23-24, 38,97-98,103-105, 130,147-148,160)

C) Trust God for your daily needs (Col. 2:6-8, Living Bible)

D) Allow the Holy Spirit to control and direct you (Acts 1:8; Eph. 5:18; Gal. 5:16,17 and 22, 23)

E) Become part of a caring Christian fellowship (Heb 10:25; Acts 2:42)

F) Let God's love flow through you (John 13:34,35- I John 4:7-21; Eph. 4:32)

G) Be obedient to His teachings (I John 2:3-6, 9-10 15-16, 29, 3:7-9, 22-4; Eph. 4:26-27; Col. 3:15-17; Gal. 5:16-18,6:1-9)

H) Learn who you are in Christ and your spiritual authority (I John 4:4; Eph. 1:3, 11, 13-14, 18, 2:6 10 18-19, 3:12,16-20, 6:10-18; Phil. 3:10, 4:13, 19; Col. 3:10; II Cor. 10:3-5; Gal. 2:20, 3:14, 26, 29)

*Healing Where You Hurt*

*Appendix C*

# FOR ADDITIONAL RESOURCES

Please refer to our website, http://www.joneargleministries.org for further information and help.

## End Notes

### Chapter 1

- Neither Tommy Tyson nor Francis MacNutt had any idea of what had happened to me, and had done nothing intentionally to hurt me. God simply was using their teaching to speak to me.

- I have never heard God speak in an audible voice, but we talk all the time, and I know what he is saying— most of the time.

### Chapter 3

- The story is true but the name and certain details have been altered.
- None of These Diseases, p. 59.
- None of These Diseases, p. 61.

### Chapter 5

- A fictitious name
- (1) They don't deserve it. (2) I don't feel like it. (3) Desire for revenge.

### Chapter 6

- Eargle paraphrase.
- Demon possession involves effective control by spirits in both the soul and spirit areas. When we are born again, our spirit is effectively removed from Satan's reach; thus, spirit problems for a believer involve only the soul (mind) arena.
- See Appendix A in the back of this book.

### Chapter 7

- *See the Inner Healing Glossary in the back of this book.
- *See Appendix B for step-by-step directions

www.ingramcontent.com/pod-product-compliance
Lightning Source LLC
Chambersburg PA
CBHW050556300426
44112CB00013B/1947